Introduction

I never get tired of designing and knitting socks. Occasionally I wander off and design other things but I still think about socks while I'm doing it – trying to work out how I can adapt the stitch pattern I'm using for this hat or shawl to a pair of socks; thinking about knitting socks in the colour of the yarn I'm currently using for something else; or an idea hits me, seemingly out of nowhere, and I have to scribble it down for later. I don't think my obsession with socks will ever stop.

The inspiration for a lot of the designs in this book began with the beautiful colours of the yarns. I love all kinds of colour – from eye-searing neons to delicate, muted pastels. The great thing about socks is that you can knit them in any colour. Amazing sock yarn is available in pretty much every shade imaginable and a colour you might not want next to your face will be fine all the way down there on your feet.

Since **Coop Knits Socks Volume 1** was published, many people have shown me their feet, clad in finished socks from the book, either in person at knitting events or online on Ravelry, Twitter or Instagram, I absolutely love seeing them so long may this continue!

Rachel x

4

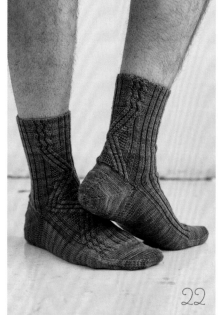

22

34

10

28

40

16

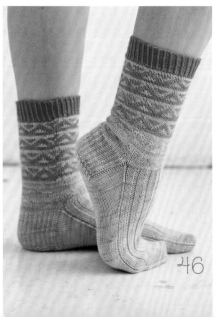

46

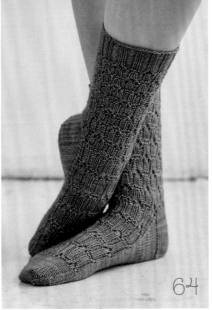

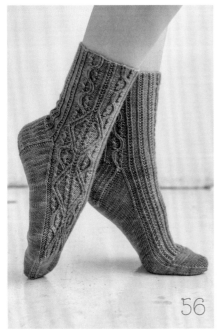

Contents

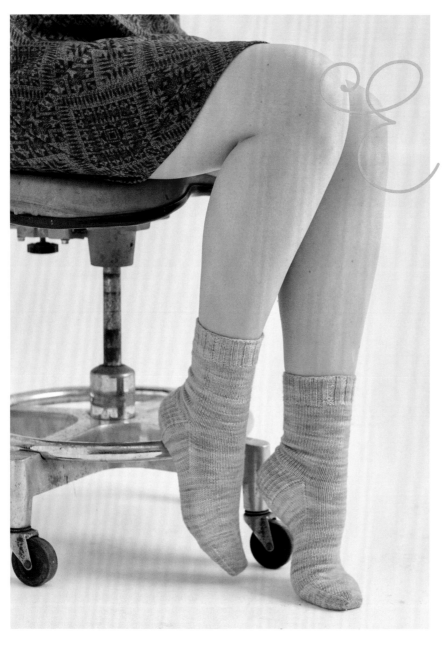

verybody knows a Dave, and everyone needs some plain Dave socks! These can be worked with either a heel flap or afterthought heel.

a sock named Dave

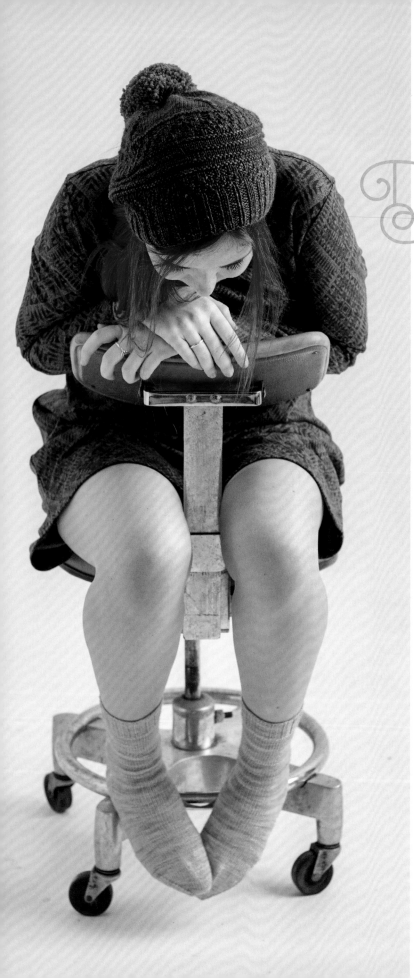

Dave

YARN
Another Crafty Girl Merino Sock (100% superwash merino; 366m [400yds] per 100g skein) 1 skein in Citrus
Small quantity of smooth 4ply waste yarn (for afterthought heel version only)

NEEDLES
2.5mm [UK 13-12/US 1-2] 80cm [32in] circular needles or DPNs (or size needed to get correct tension)
Stitch markers
Tapestry needle

TENSION
36 sts and 50 rounds = 10cm [4in] over st st

SIZES
Small (Medium, Large)
To fit foot circumference: 20.5 (23, 25.5) cm [8 (9, 10) in]
Actual foot circumference of sock (unstretched): 18 (20.5, 23) cm [7 (8, 9) in]
Length of leg to top of heel flap: 15cm [6in]
Foot length is fully adjustable within the pattern.
Finished sock measures 0.5cm [¼in] less than actual foot length, to ensure a good fit.

PATTERN NOTES
The pattern gives instructions for a heel flap and an afterthought heel version of these socks. The heel flap version is shown in the photographs.

ABBREVIATIONS
See full list of abbreviations on page 84.

The Percy Hat worn by Caroline is also one of Rachel's designs, available from www.coopknits.co.uk

HEEL FLAP VERSION

CUFF

Cast on 64 (72, 80) sts. Join to work in the round, being careful not to twist. Place marker for start of round.

Round 1: *K1, p2, k1; rep from * to end. Work this round a further 19 times (20 rounds).

LEG

Rounds 1-54: Knit.

HEEL FLAP

Turn work so WS is facing. Heel flap will be worked back and forth on the next 32 (36, 40) sts, beginning with a WS row. Keep remaining 32 (36, 40) sts on needles for instep.

Row 1 (WS): Sl1 wyif, p31 (35, 39).
Row 2 (RS): *Sl1 wyib, k1; rep from * to end. Rep these 2 rows a further 14 times, then work row 1 once more.

HEEL TURN

Row 1 (RS): Sl1 wyib, k18 (20, 22), ssk, k1, turn, leaving remaining 10 (12, 14) sts unworked.
Row 2 (WS): Sl1 wyif, p7, p2tog, p1, turn, leaving remaining 10 (12, 14) sts unworked.
Row 3: Sl1 wyib, knit to 1 st before gap, ssk, k1, turn.
Row 4: Sl1 wyif, purl to 1 st before gap, p2tog, p1, turn.
Rep last 2 rows a further 4 (5, 6) times. All heel sts have been worked. 20 (22, 24) heel sts remain.

GUSSET

Begin working in the round again as follows:

Set-up round: Sl1, k19 (21, 23), pick up and knit 16 sts along edge of heel flap (1 st in each slipped st along edge of the flap), k32 (36, 40) across instep sts, pick up and knit 16 sts along edge of heel flap, k36 (38, 40). Place marker for new start of round (at start of instep sts). 84 (90, 96) sts.

Round 1: K32 (36, 40), ssk, knit to 2 sts before end of round, k2tog. 2 sts dec.
Round 2: Knit.
Last 2 rounds set gusset decreases. Rep these 2 rounds a further 9 (8, 7) times. 20 (18, 16) sts dec; 64 (72, 80) sts remain. You now have 32 (36, 40) sts each on instep and sole.

FOOT

Work st st in the round (knit every round) as set until the sock measures 5 (5.5, 6) cm [2 (2, 2½) in] less than the desired foot length.

TOE

Round 1: K1, ssk, k26 (30, 34), k2tog, k1, pm, k1, ssk, knit to last 3 sts, k2tog, k1. 60 (68, 76) sts.
Round 2: Knit.
Round 3: *K1, ssk, knit to 3 sts before marker, k2tog, k1, slm; rep from * once more. 4 sts dec.
Rep last 2 rounds a further 9 (10, 12) times. 40 (44, 52) sts dec; 20 (24, 24) sts remain.
Cut yarn, leaving a 30cm [12in] tail. Graft sts together using Kitchener stitch. Weave in ends.

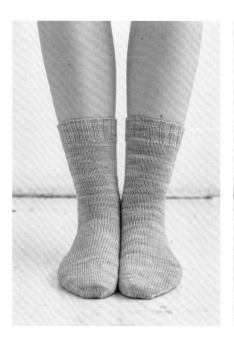
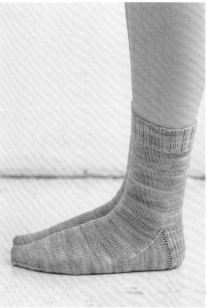
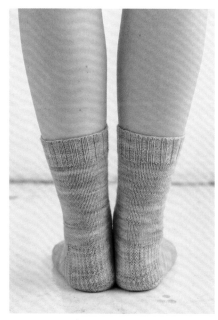

AFTERTHOUGHT HEEL VERSION

CUFF AND LEG
Work as Heel Flap version.

HEEL SET-UP
Next round: K32 (36, 40), use a length of waste yarn to knit 32 (36, 40) sts to end of round. Slip these 32 (36, 40) sts back on to left needle and then knit them again with the working yarn.

You now have 32 (36, 40) sts of waste yarn in your fabric. After completion of the toe, you will return to these sts, unpick the waste yarn and work an 'afterthought' heel.

FOOT
Continue to work in st st as set until sock measures 10.5 (11.5, 12.5) cm [4 (4½, 5) in] less than the desired foot length when measured from the row of waste yarn sts.

TOE
Work as Heel Flap version.

AFTERTHOUGHT HEEL
Pick up the right leg (or side) of the 32 (36, 40) main yarn sts under the row of waste yarn sts. Turn the sock and rep the process again, picking up 32 (36, 40) sts from the other side of the waste yarn. You now have 64 (72, 80) sts on your needles. Carefully remove the waste yarn, ensuring all sts are safely on your needles. Begin to work in the round as follows:

Round 1: K32 (36, 40), pick up and knit 2 sts in the gap between the sole and instep, k32 (36, 40), pick up and knit 2 sts in the gap between the sole and instep, place marker for start of round. 68 (76, 84) sts.

SMALL SIZE ONLY
Round 2: *K32, k2tog; rep from * once more. 66 sts.

MEDIUM SIZE ONLY
Round 2: *K17, k2tog; rep from * to end. 72 sts.

LARGE SIZE ONLY
Round 2: Knit. 84 sts.

ALL SIZES
Knit 8 rounds.

SHAPE HEEL
LARGE SIZE ONLY
Round 1: *K12, k2tog; rep from * to end. 78 sts.
Round 2: Knit.
Round 3: *K11, k2tog; rep from * to end. 72 sts.
Round 4: Knit.

LARGE AND MEDIUM SIZES
Round 5: *K10, k2tog; rep from * to end. 66 sts.
Round 6: Knit.

ALL SIZES
Round 7: *K9, k2tog; rep from * to end. 60 sts.
Round 8: Knit.
Round 9: *K8, k2tog; rep from * to end. 54 sts.
Round 10: Knit.
Round 11: *K7, k2tog; rep from * to end. 48 sts.
Round 12: Knit.
Round 13: *K6, k2tog; rep from * to end. 42 sts.
Round 14: Knit.
Round 15: *K5, k2tog; rep from * to end. 36 sts.
Round 16: Knit.
Round 17: *K4, k2tog; rep from * to end. 30 sts.
Round 18: Knit.
Round 19: *K3, k2tog; rep from * to end. 24 sts.
Round 20: Knit.

Round 21: *K2, K2tog; rep from * to end. 18 sts.
Round 22: *K1, K2tog; rep from * to end. 12 sts.
Round 23: *K2tog; rep from * to end. 6 sts.

Break the yarn, leaving a 15cm [6in] tail, thread tail through the remaining sts and pull tightly to close the heel. Weave in the ends.

Sock it to me, Eugene

Worked in a super-stretchy textured stitch pattern, these Eugene socks will keep your feet toasty.

Eugene

YARN
Whimsy Sokkusu O (100% superwash merino; 380m [415 yds] per 115g skein)
1 skein in Fall Foliage

NEEDLES
2.5mm [UK 13-12/US 1-2] 80cm [32in] circular needles or DPNs (or size needed to get correct tension)
Stitch markers
Tapestry needle

TENSION
36 sts and 50 rounds = 10cm [4in] over st st
46 sts and 50 rounds = 10cm [4in] over leg and foot stitch patterns (unstretched)

SIZES
Small (Medium, Large)
To fit foot circumference: 20.5 (23, 25.5) cm [8 (9, 10) in]
Actual foot circumference of sock (unstretched): 16 (18, 20.5) cm [6¼ (7¼, 8) in]
Length of leg to top of heel flap: 15cm [6in]
Foot length is fully adjustable within the pattern.
Finished sock measures 0.5cm [¼in] less than actual foot length, to ensure a good fit.

PATTERN NOTES
The charted stitch patterns are also given as written instructions at the end of the pattern.

ABBREVIATIONS
m1l: Pick up the strand between stitches from front to back and knit through the back of this loop. 1 stitch increased.
m1r: Pick up the strand between stitches from back to front and knit this loop. 1 stitch increased.
m1 purlwise: Pick up the strand between stitches from front to back and purl through the back of this loop. 1 stitch increased.
See full list of abbreviations on page 84.

Sigorni is wearing a beautiful hand-knit Strokkur sweater, designed by Ysolda Teague.

SOCK ONE

CUFF AND LEG

Cast on 64 (72, 80) sts. Join to work in the round, being careful not to twist. Place marker for start of round.

Rounds 1-18: *P1, k2, p1; rep from * to end.

Rounds 19-22: *K1, p2, k1; rep from * to end.

Rounds 23-26: *P1, k2, p1; rep from * to end.

Rounds 27-30: Rep rounds 19-22.

Rounds 31-40: *P1, k2, p1; rep from * to end.

Work rounds 19-40 once more.

Work rounds 19-30 once more (74 rounds).

HEEL FLAP

Turn work so WS is facing. Heel flap will be worked back and forth on the next 32 (36, 40) sts, beginning with a WS row. Keep remaining 32 (36, 40) sts on needles for instep.

Row 1 (WS): Sl1 wyif, p31 (35, 39).
Row 2 (RS): *Sl1 wyib, k1; rep from * to end.
Rep these 2 rows a further 14 times, then work row 1 once more.

HEEL TURN

Row 1 (RS): Sl1 wyib, k18 (20, 22), ssk, k1, turn, leaving remaining 10 (12, 14) sts unworked.
Row 2 (WS): Sl1 wyif, p7, p2tog, p1, turn, leaving remaining 10 (12, 14) sts unworked.
Row 3: Sl1 wyib, knit to 1 st before gap, ssk, k1, turn.
Row 4: Sl1 wyif, purl to 1 st before gap, p2tog, p1, turn.
Rep last 2 rows 4 (5, 6) more times. All heel sts have been worked. 20 (22, 24) heel sts remain.

GUSSET

Begin working in the round again as follows:
Set-up round: Sl1 wyib, k19 (21, 23), pick up and knit 16 sts along edge of heel flap (1 st in each slipped st along edge of flap), work across 32 (36, 40) instep sts as foll: reading from right to left, work across row 1 of chart A, rep sts outlined in red 6 (7, 8) times in total before completing the row, pick up and knit 16 sts along edge of heel flap, k36 (38, 40). Place marker for new start of round (at start of instep sts). 84 (90, 96) sts.

Round 1: Work in pattern from row 2 of chart A, rep sts outlined in red 6 (7, 8) times in total, before completing the row, ssk, knit to last 2 sts, k2tog. 2 sts dec.
Round 2: Work in pattern from row 3 of chart A, rep sts outlined in red 6 (7, 8) times in total, before completing the row, knit to end.
Working next row of chart each time, rep last 2 rounds a further 9 (8, 7) times. 20 (18, 16) sts dec; 64 (72, 80) sts remain. You now have 32 (36, 40) sts each on instep and sole.

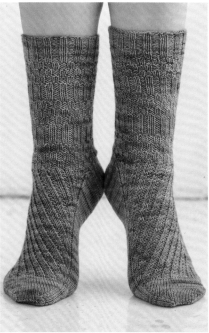

Eugene

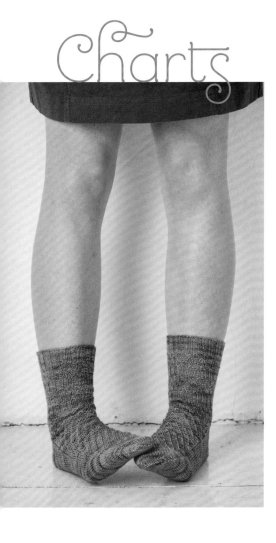

Charts

KEY

☐ knit

⦿ purl

◢ ssk

◣ k2tog

Ⓜ m1l

ⓂR m1r

Ⓜ m1 purlwise

☐ pattern repeat

CHART B

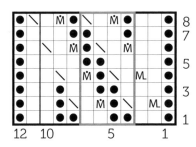

12 10   5   1

CHART A

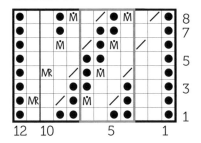

12 10   5   1

Pattern continues:

FOOT
Work as set (chart A on instep and st st on sole) until the sock measures 5 (5.5, 6.5) cm [2 (2¼, 2½) in] less than the desired foot length.

TOE
Round 1: Knit.
Round 2: K1, ssk, k26 (30, 34), k2tog, k1, pm, k1, ssk, knit to last 3 sts, k2tog, k1. 60 (68, 76) sts.
Round 3: Knit.
Round 4: *K1, ssk, knit to 3 sts before marker, k2tog, k1, slm; rep from * once more. 4 sts dec.
Rep last 2 rounds a further 9 (10, 12) times. 40 (44, 52) sts dec; 20 (24, 24) sts remain.
Cut yarn, leaving a 30cm [12in] tail. Graft sts together using Kitchener stitch. Weave in ends.

SOCK TWO

CUFF, LEG, HEEL FLAP AND TURN
Work as Sock One.

GUSSET AND FOOT
Work as for Sock One, using chart B instead of chart A.

TOE
Work as Sock One.

Eugene

WRITTEN CHART INSTRUCTIONS

CHART A

MULTIPLE OF 4 + 8 STS AND 8 ROUNDS

Rep instructions from * to * as indicated in the pattern.

Round 1: P1, k2, *p2, k2*, p2, k2, p1.
Round 2: P1, k2, *p1, k2tog, k1, m1 purlwise*, p1, k2tog, k1, m1r, p1.
Round 3: P1, k2, *p1, k2, p1*, p1, k3, p1.
Round 4: P1, k2, *k2tog, k1, m1 purlwise, p1*, k2tog, k1, m1r, k1, p1.
Round 5: P1, k2, *k2, p2*, k4, p1.
Round 6: P1, k1, k2tog, *k1, m1 purlwise, p1, k2tog*, k1, m1 purlwise, k2, p1.
Round 7: P1, k2, *k1, p2, k1*, k1, p1, k2, p1.
Round 8: P1, k2tog, k1, *m1 purlwise, p1, k2tog, k1*, m1 purlwise, p1, k2, p1.

CHART B

MULTIPLE OF 4 + 8 STS AND 8 ROUNDS

Rep instructions from * to * as indicated in the pattern.

Round 1: P1, k2, *p2, k2*, p2, k2, p1.
Round 2: P1, m1l, k1, *ssk, p1, m1 purlwise, k1*, ssk, p1, k2, p1.
Round 3: P1, k2, *k1, p2, k1*, k1, p1, k2, p1.
Round 4: P1, k1, m1l, *k1, ssk, p1, m1 purlwise*, k1, ssk, k2, p1.
Round 5: P1, k2, *k2, p2*, k4, p1.
Round 6: P1, k2, *m1 purlwise, k1, ssk, p1*, m1 purlwise, k1, ssk, k1, p1.
Round 7: P1, k2, *p1, k2, p1*, p1, k3, p1.
Round 8: P1, k2, *p1, m1 purlwise, k1, ssk*, p1, m1 purlwise, k1, ssk, p1.

Phyllis on my feet!

Sharply defined travelling twisted stitches create the diamond patterns that track along the length of these socks.

Phyllis

YARN
Kettle Yarn Co Twist (100% British Superwash Bluefaced Leicester; 183m [200yds] per 50g skein) 2 skeins in Canal

NEEDLES
2.5mm [UK 13-12/US 1-2] 80cm [32in] circular needles or DPNs (or size needed to get correct tension)
Cable needle
Stitch markers
Tapestry needle

TENSION
36 sts and 50 rounds = 10cm [4in] over st st
30 sts = 7cm [2¾in] over chart cable pattern
36 rounds = 8.5cm [3¼in] over chart cable pattern (2 repeats)

SIZES
Small (Medium, Large)
To fit foot circumference: 20.5 (23, 25.5) cm [8 (9, 10) in]
Actual foot circumference of sock (unstretched): 17.5 (19.5, 21.5) cm [7 (7¾, 8½) in]
Length of leg to top of heel flap: 16cm [6¼in]
Foot length is fully adjustable within the pattern. Finished sock measures 0.5cm [¼in] less than actual foot length, to ensure a good fit.

PATTERN NOTES
The charted stitch patterns are also given as written instructions at the end of the pattern.

ABBREVIATIONS
1/1 LT: Slip next st to cable needle and place at front of work, k1tbl, then k1tbl from cable needle
1/1 RT: Slip next st to cable needle and place at back of work, k1tbl, then k1tbl from cable needle
1/1 LPT: Slip next st to cable needle and place at front of work, p1, then k1tbl from cable needle
1/1 RPT: Slip next st to cable needle and place at back of work, k1tbl, then p1 from cable needle
See full list of abbreviations on page 84.

BOTH SOCKS

CUFF

Cast on 70 (78, 86) sts. Join to work in the round, being careful not to twist. Place marker for start of round.

Round 1: [P1, k1tbl] 1 (2, 3) times, *p2, k1tbl, p1, k1tbl, p4, k1tbl, p1, k1tbl, p2, k2tbl, p2, k1tbl, p1, k1tbl, p4, k1tbl, p1, k1tbl, p2*, [k1tbl, p1] 2 (4, 6) times, k1tbl, work from * to * once more, [k1tbl, p1] 1 (2, 3) times, k1tbl.
Rep last round 15 more times (16 rounds).

LEG

Round 1: [P1, k1tbl] 1 (2, 3) times, reading from right to left, work 30 sts from row 1 of chart A, [k1tbl, p1] 2 (4, 6) times, k1tbl, work 30 sts from row 1 of chart A, [k1tbl, p1] 1 (2, 3) times, k1tbl.
Working next row of chart A each time, continue in pattern as set until chart A has been completed 3 times (54 rounds).

HEEL FLAP

Turn work so WS is facing. Heel flap will be worked back and forth on the next 36 (40, 44) beginning with a WS row. Keep remaining 34 (38, 42) sts on needles for instep.

Row 1 (WS): Sl1 wyif, p35 (39, 43).
Row 2 (RS): *Sl1 wyib, k1; rep from * to end.
Rep these 2 rows a further 14 times, then work row 1 once more.

HEEL TURN

Row 1 (RS): Sl1 wyib, k20 (22, 24), ssk, k1, turn, leaving remaining 12 (14, 16) sts unworked.
Row 2 (WS): Sl1 wyif, p7, p2tog, p1, turn, leaving remaining 12 (14, 16) sts unworked.
Row 3: Sl1 wyib, knit to 1 st before gap, ssk, k1, turn.
Row 4: Sl1 wyif, purl to 1 st before gap, p2tog, p1, turn.

Rep last 2 rows a further 5 (6, 7) times. All heel sts have been worked. 22 (24, 26) heel sts remain.

GUSSET

Begin working in the round again as follows:

Set-up round: Sl1 wyib, k21 (23, 25), pick up and knit 16 sts along edge of heel flap (1 st in each slipped st along edge of flap), work across 34 (38, 42) instep sts as follows: [P1, k1tbl] 1 (2, 3) times, reading from right to left, work from row 1 of chart A, [k1tbl, p1] 1 (2, 3) times, pick up and knit 16 sts along edge of heel flap, k38 (40, 42). Place marker for new start of round (at start of instep sts). 88 (94, 100) sts.

Round 1: Work in pattern as set over 34 (38, 42) instep sts, (chart A and twisted rib as established), ssk, knit to last 2 sts, k2tog. 2 sts dec.
Round 2: Work in pattern as set over 34 (38, 42) instep sts, (chart A and twisted rib as established), knit to end.

Phyllis

Charts

Pattern continues:

Working next row of chart A each time, rep last 2 rounds a further 9 (8, 7) times. 20 (18, 16) sts dec; 68 (76, 84) sts remain.

You now have 34 (38, 42) sts each on instep and sole.

FOOT

Work as set (chart A and twisted rib on instep and st st on sole) until the sock measures 5.5 (6, 6.5) cm [2¼ (2¼, 2½) in] less than the desired foot length.

TOE

Round 1: Knit.
Round 2: K1, ssk, k28 (32, 36), k2tog, k1, pm, k1, ssk, knit to last 3 sts, k2tog, k1. 64 (72, 80) sts.
Round 3: Knit.
Round 4: *K1, ssk, knit to 3 sts before marker, k2tog, k1, slm; rep from * once more. 4 sts dec.
Rep last 2 rounds a further 10 (11, 13) times. 44 (48, 56) sts dec; 20 (24, 24) sts remain.
Cut yarn, leaving a 30cm [12in] tail. Graft sts together using Kitchener stitch. Weave in ends.

KEY

☐ knit

⬤ purl

𝑅 k1tbl

1/1 LT: Slip next st to cable needle and place at front of work, k1tbl, then k1tbl from cable needle.

1/1 RT: Slip next st to cable needle and place at back of work, k1tbl, then k1tbl from cable needle.

1/1 LPT: Slip next st to cable needle and place at front of work, p1, then k1tbl from cable needle.

1/1 RPT: Slip next st to cable needle and place at back of work, k1tbl, then p1 from cable needle.

The colourful blanket that Caroline is snuggled on was found in a local charity shop so, sadly, we aren't able to give you the pattern details.

CHART A

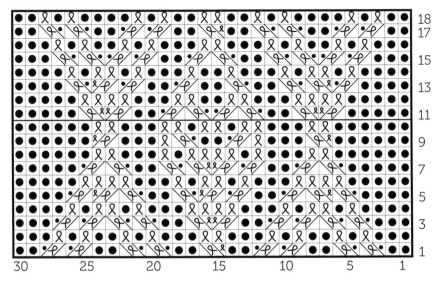

Phyllis

WRITTEN CHART INSTRUCTIONS

CHART A

30 STS AND 18 ROUNDS

Round 1: P2, [1/1 LPT] twice, p2, [1/1 RPT] twice, p2, 1/1 LT, p2, [1/1 LPT] twice, p2, [1/1 RPT] twice, p2.

Round 2: P3, k1tbl, p1, k1tbl, p2, k1tbl, p1, k1tbl, p3, k2tbl, p3, k1tbl, p1, k1tbl, p2, k1tbl, p1, k1tbl, p3.

Round 3: P3, [1/1 LPT] twice, [1/1 RPT] twice, p2, 1/1 RT, 1/1 LT, p2, [1/1 LPT] twice, [1/1 RPT] twice, p3.

Round 4: P4, k1tbl, p1, k2tbl, p1, k1tbl, p3, k4tbl, p3, k1tbl, p1, k2tbl, p1, k1tbl, p4.

Round 5: P4, 1/1 LPT, 1/1 LT, 1/1 RPT, p2, 1/1 RPT, 1/1 RT, 1/1 LPT, p2, 1/1 LPT, 1/1 RT, 1/1 RPT, p4.

Round 6: P5, k4tbl, p3, k1tbl, p1, k2tbl, p1, k1tbl, p3, k4tbl, p5.

Round 7: P5, 1/1 LPT, 1/1 RPT, p2, 1/1 RPT, 1/1 RT, 1/1 LT, 1/1 LPT, p2, 1/1 LPT, 1/1 RPT, p5.

Round 8: P6, k2tbl, p3, k1tbl, p1, k4tbl, p1, k1tbl, p3, k2tbl, p6.

Round 9: P6, 1/1 LT, p3, k1tbl, 1/1 RPT, p2, 1/1 LPT, k1tbl, p3, 1/1 RT, p6.

Round 10: P6, k2tbl, p3, [k2tbl, p1] twice, k2tbl, p3, k2tbl, p6.

Round 11: P5, 1/1 RT, 1/1 LT, p2, [1/1 LPT, 1/1 RPT] twice, p2, 1/1 RT, 1/1 LT, p5.

Round 12: P5, k4tbl, p3, k2tbl, p2, k2tbl, p3, k4tbl, p5.

Round 13: P4, 1/1 RPT, 1/1 LT, [1/1 LPT, p2] twice, 1/1 RPT, p2, 1/1 RPT, 1/1 RT, 1/1 LPT, p4.

Round 14: P4, k1tbl, p1, k2tbl, p1, k1tbl, p3, k1tbl, p2, k1tbl, p3, k1tbl, p1, k2tbl, p1, k1tbl, p4.

Round 15: P3, [1/1 RPT] twice, [1/1 LPT] twice, p2, 1/1 LPT, 1/1 RPT, p2, [1/1 RPT] twice, [1/1 LPT] twice, p3.

Round 16: Repeat round 2.

Round 17: P2, [1/1 RPT] twice, p2, [1/1 LPT] twice, p2, 1/1 LT, p2, [1/1 RPT] twice, p2, [1/1 LPT] twice, p2.

Round 18: P2, k1tbl, p1, k1tbl, p4, k1tbl, p1, k1tbl, p2, k2tbl, p2, k1tbl, p1, k1tbl, p4, k1tbl, p1, k1tbl, p2.

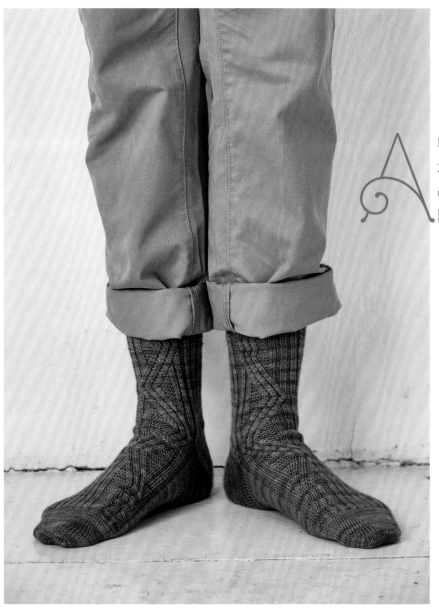

An afterthought heel and zigzagging rib pattern creates a pair of socks to love or for your love.

Orville

loves socks

Orville

TENSION
36 sts and 50 rounds = 10cm [4in] over st st
22 sts = 5cm [2in] over chart cable pattern
48 rounds = 10cm [4in] over chart cable pattern

SIZES
Small (Medium, Large)
To fit foot circumference: 20.5 (23, 25.5) cm [8 (9, 10) in]
Actual foot circumference of sock (unstretched): 18 (20.5, 22.5) cm [7 (8, 9) in]
Length of leg to top of heel flap: 16cm [6¼in]
Foot length is fully adjustable within the pattern.
Finished sock measures 0.5cm [¼in] less than actual foot length, to ensure a good fit.

PATTERN NOTES
The charted stitch patterns are also given as written instructions at the end of the pattern.

ABBREVIATIONS
2/1 LC: Slip next 2 sts to cable needle and place at front of work, k1, then k2 from cable needle
2/1 RC: Slip next st to cable needle and place at back of work, k2, then k1 from cable needle
2/1 LPC: Slip next 2 sts to cable needle and place at front of work, p1, then k2 from cable needle
2/1 RPC: Slip next st to cable needle and place at back of work, k2, then p1 from cable needle
See full list of abbreviations on page 84.

SOCK ONE

CUFF
Cast on 68 (76, 84) sts. Join to work in the round, being careful not to twist. Place marker for start of round.

Rounds 1 and 2: *P4, [k2, p2] 3 times, p4, [k2, p2] 3 (4, 5) times, k2; rep from * once more.
Round 3: *P4, reading from right to left, work 12 sts from row 1 of chart A, p4, [k2, p2] 3 (4, 5) times, k2; rep from * once more.
Last round sets chart A and rib patterns. Working next row of chart A each time, continue in pattern as set until Chart A has been completed 3 times (24 chart A rounds; 26 rounds total).

YARN
Silver Version: Lornas Laces Solemate (55% merino, 30% rayon, 15% nylon; 389m [425yds] per 100g skein) 1 skein in Dobson
Green Version: Easyknits Deeply Wicked (100% superwash merino; 400m [437yds] per 100g skein) 1 skein in Moira
Small quantity of smooth 4ply waste yarn.

NEEDLES
2.5mm [UK 13-12/US 1-2] 80cm [32in] circular needles or DPNs (or size needed to get correct tension)
Cable needle
Stitch markers
Tapestry needle

LEG

Round 27: *P4, reading from right to left, work 22 sts from row 1 of chart B, [p2, k2] 2 (3, 4) times; rep from * once more. Last round sets chart B and rib patterns. Work as set until chart B has been completed once (24 rounds).

Round 51: *P4, reading from right to left, work 22 sts from row 1 of chart C, [p2, k2] 2 (3, 4) times; rep from * once more. Last round sets chart C and rib patterns. Work as set until chart C has been completed once (24 rounds).

HEEL SET-UP

Round 75: P4, work 22 sts from row 1 of chart B, [p2, k2] 2 (3, 4) times, use a piece of waste yarn to knit 34 (38, 42) sts to end of round. Slip these 34 (38, 42) sts back on to left needle and then knit them again with the working yarn.

You now have 34 (38, 42) sts of waste yarn in your fabric. After completion of the toe, you will return to these sts, unpick the waste yarn and work an 'afterthought' heel.

FOOT

Round 76: P4, work 22 sts from row 2 of chart B, [p2, k2] 2 (3, 4) times, knit to end. Last round sets chart B and rib on instep, and st st on sole. Continue to work as set until chart B is complete.

Round 99: P4, work 22 sts from row 1 of chart C, [p2, k2] 2 (3, 4) times, knit to end. Last round sets chart C and rib on instep, and st st on sole. Continue to work as set until chart C is complete.

Round 123: P4, work 12 sts from row 1 of chart A, p4, [k2, p2] 3 (4, 5) times, k2, knit to end. Last round sets chart A and rib on instep, and st st on sole. Continue to work as set until sock measures 11.5 (12, 13.5) cm [4½ (4¾, 5¼) in] less than the desired foot length when measured from the row of waste yarn sts.

TOE

Round 1: Knit.
Round 2: K1, ssk, k28 (32, 36), k2tog, k1, pm, k1, ssk, knit to last 3 sts, k2tog, k1. 64 (72, 80) sts.
Round 3: Knit.
Round 4: *K1, ssk, knit to 3 sts before marker, k2tog, k1, slm; rep from * once more. 4 sts dec.
Rep last 2 rounds a further 10 (11, 13) times. 44 (48, 56) sts dec; 20 (24, 24) sts remain. Cut yarn, leaving a 30cm [12in] tail. Graft sts together using Kitchener stitch. Weave in ends.

AFTERTHOUGHT HEEL

Pick up the right leg (or side) of the 34 (38, 42) main yarn sts under the row of waste yarn sts. Turn the sock and rep the process again, picking up 34 (38, 42) sts from the other side of the waste yarn. You now have 68 (76, 84) sts on your needles. Carefully remove the waste yarn, ensuring all sts are safely on your needles. Begin to work in the round as follows:

Round 1: K34 (38, 42), pick up and knit 2 sts in the gap between the sole and instep, k34 (38, 42), pick up and knit 2 sts in the gap between the sole and instep and place marker for start of round. 72 (80, 88) sts.

SMALL SIZE ONLY
Round 2: Knit. 72 sts.

MEDIUM SIZE ONLY
Round 2: *K38, k2tog; rep from * once more. 78 sts.

LARGE SIZE ONLY
Round 2: *K20, k2tog; rep from * to end of round. 84 sts.

ALL SIZES
Knit 8 rounds.

SHAPE HEEL
LARGE SIZE ONLY
Round 1: *K12, k2tog; rep from * to end. 78 sts.
Round 2: Knit.

LARGE AND MEDIUM SIZES
Round 3: * K11, k2tog; rep from * to end. 72 sts.
Round 4: Knit.

ALL SIZES
Round 5: * K10, k2tog; rep from * to end. 66 sts.
Round 6: Knit.
Round 7: *K9, k2tog; rep from * to end. 60 sts.
Round 8: Knit.
Round 9: *K8, k2tog; rep from * to end. 54 sts.
Round 10: Knit.
Round 11: *K7, k2tog; rep from * to end. 48 sts.
Round 12: Knit.
Round 13: *K6, k2tog; rep from * to end. 42 sts.

Orville

Charts

Pattern continues:

Round 14: Knit.
Round 15: *K5, k2tog; rep from * to end. 36 sts.
Round 16: Knit.
Round 17: *K4, k2tog; rep from * to end. 30 sts.
Round 18: Knit.
Round 19: *K3, k2tog; rep from * to end. 24 sts.
Round 20: Knit.
Round 21: *K2, K2tog; rep from * to end. 18 sts.
Round 22: *K1, K2tog; rep from * to end. 12 sts.
Round 23: *K2tog; rep from * to end. 6 sts.

Break the yarn, leaving a 15cm [6in] tail, thread tail through the remaining sts and pull tightly to close the heel.
Weave in the ends.

SOCK TWO

Cast on 68 (76, 84) sts. Join to work in the round, being careful not to twist. Place marker for start of round.

Rounds 1 and 2: K2, [p2, k2] 3 (4, 5) times, p4, [p2, k2] 3 times, p4; rep from * once more.

KEY

☐ knit

⦿ purl

⧅ **2/1 LC:** Slip next 2 sts to cable needle and place at front of work, k1, then k2 from cable needle.

⧅ **2/1 RC:** Slip next st to cable needle and place at back of work, k2, then k1 from cable needle.

⧅ **2/1 LPC:** Slip next 2 sts to cable needle and place at front of work, p1, then k2 from cable needle.

⧅ **2/1 RPC:** Slip next st to cable needle and place at back of work, k2, then p1 from cable needle.

CHART C

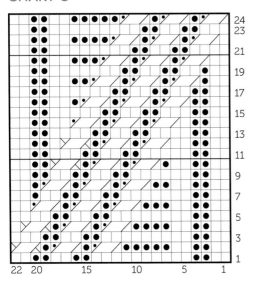

CHART B

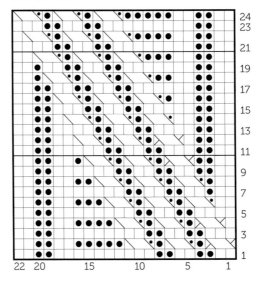

CHART A

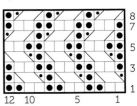

Round 3: *K2, [p2, k2] 3 (4, 5) times, p4, work 12 sts from **row 5** of chart A, p4; rep from * once more.
Last round sets chart A and rib patterns. Work as set until row 4 of chart A is complete for the third time (24 rounds).

LEG

Round 27: *[K2, p2] 2 (3, 4) times, work 22 sts from row 1 of chart C, p4; rep from * once more.
Last round sets chart C and rib patterns. Work as set until chart C has been completed once (24 rounds).

Round 51: *[K2, p2] 2 (3, 4) times, work 22 sts from row 1 of chart B, p4; rep from * once more.
Last round sets chart B and rib patterns. Work as set until chart B has been completed once (24 rounds).

HEEL SET-UP

Round 75: [K2, p2] 2 (3, 4) times, work 22 sts from row 1 of chart C, p4, use a piece of waste yarn to knit 34 (38, 42) sts to end of round. Slip these 34 (38, 42) sts back on to left needle and then knit them again with the working yarn.

You now have 34 (38, 42) sts of waste yarn in your fabric. After completion of the toe, you will return to these sts, unpick the waste yarn and work an 'afterthought' heel.

FOOT

Round 76: *[K2, p2] 2 (3, 4) times, work 22 sts from row 2 of chart C, p4, knit to end.
Last round sets chart C and rib on instep, and st st on sole. Continue to work as set until chart C is complete.

Round 99: *[K2, p2] 2 (3, 4) times, work 22 sts from row 1 of chart B, p4, knit to end.
Last round sets chart B and rib on instep, and st st on sole. Continue to work as set until chart B is complete.

Round 123: K2, [p2, k2] 3 (4, 5) times, p4, work 12 sts from row 5 of chart A, p4, knit to end.

Last round sets chart A and rib on instep, and st st on sole. Continue to work as set until sock measures 11.5 (12, 13.5) cm [4½ (4¾, 5¼) in] less than the desired foot length when measured from the row of waste yarn sts.

TOE AND HEEL

Work as Sock One.

WRITTEN CHART INSTRUCTIONS

CHART A

12 STS AND 8 ROUNDS
Round 1: [K2, p2] 3 times.
Round 2: [2/1 LPC, p1] 3 times.
Round 3: P1, [k2, p2] twice, k2, p1.
Round 4: [P1, 2/1 LPC] 3 times.
Round 5: [P2, k2] 3 times.
Round 6: [P1, 2/1 RPC] 3 times.
Round 7: Rep round 3.
Round 8: [2/1 RPC, p1] 3 times.

CHART B

22 STS AND 24 ROUNDS
Round 1: [K2, p2] twice, k10, p2, k2.
Round 2: 2/1 LC, [p1, 2/1 LPC] twice, p5, k2, p2, k2.
Round 3: K3, p2, k2, p2, k9, p2, k2.
Round 4: K1, 2/1 LC, [p1, 2/1 LPC] twice, p4, k2, p2, k2.
Round 5: K4, p2, k2, k2, k8, p2, k2.
Round 6: K2, [2/1 LPC, p1] twice, 2/1 LPC, p3, k2, p2, k2.
Round 7: K2, p1, [k2, p2] twice, k7, p2, k2.
Round 8: K2, [p1, 2/1 LPC] 3 times, [p2, k2] twice.
Round 9: [K2, p2] 3 times, k6, p2, k2.
Round 10: K2, p2, 2/1 LC, [p1, 2/1 LPC] twice, p1, k2, p2, k2.
Round 11: K2, p2, k3, p2, k2, p2, k5, p2, k2.
Round 12: K2, p2, k1, 2/1 LC, [p1, 2/1 LPC] twice, k2, p2, k2.
Round 13: [K2, p2, k4, p2] twice, k2.
Round 14: K2, p2, k2, [2/1 LPC, p1] twice, 2/1 LPC, k1, p2, k2.
Round 15: K2, p2, k5, p2, k2, p2, k3, p2, k2.
Round 16: K2, p2, k2, [p1, 2/1 LPC] 3 times, p2, k2.
Round 17: K2, p2, k6, [k2, p2] 3 times.

CHART C

22 STS AND 24 ROUNDS
Round 1: K2, p2, k10, [p2, k2] twice.
Round 2: K2, p2, k2, p5, [2/1 RPC, p1] twice, 2/1 RC.
Round 3: K2, p2, k9, p2, k2, p2, k3.
Round 4: K2, p2, k2, p4, [2/1 RPC, p1] twice, 2/1 RC, k1.
Round 5: K2, p2, k8, p2, k2, p2, k4.
Round 6: K2, p2, k2, p3, [2/1 RPC, p1] twice, 2/1 RPC, k2.
Round 7: K2, p2, k7, [p2, k2] twice, p1, k2.
Round 8: [K2, p2] twice, [2/1 RPC, p1] 3 times, k2.
Round 9: K2, p2, k6, [p2, k2] 3 times.
Round 10: K2, p2, k2, [p1, 2/1 RPC] twice, p1, 2/1 RC, p2, k2.
Round 11: K2, p2, k5, p2, k2, p2, k3, p2, k2.
Round 12: K2, p2, k2, [2/1 RPC, p1] twice, 2/1 RC, k1, p2, k2.
Round 13: [K2, p2, k4, p2] twice, k2.
Round 14: K2, p2, k1, [2/1 RPC, p1] twice, 2/1 RPC, k2, p2, k2.
Round 15: K2, p2, k3, p2, k2, p2, k5, p2, k2.
Round 16: K2, p2, [2/1 RPC, p1] 3 times, k2, p2, k2.
Round 17: [K2, p2] 3 times, k6, p2, k2.
Round 18: K2, [p1, 2/1 RPC] 3 times, [p2, k2] twice.
Round 19: K2, p1, [k2, p2] twice, k7, p2, k2.
Round 20: K2, [2/1 RPC, p1] twice, 2/1 RPC, p3, k2, p2, k2.
Round 21: K4, p2, k2, p2, k8, p2, k2.
Round 22: K1, [2/1 RPC, p1] twice, 2/1 RPC, p4, k2, p2, k2.
Round 23: K3, p2, k2, p2, k9, p2, k2.
Round 24: [2/1 RPC, p1] twice, 2/1 RPC, p5, k2, p2, k2.

CHART A (continued)

Round 18: [K2, p2] twice, [2/1 LPC, p1] 3 times, k2.
Round 19: K2, p2, k7, [p2, k2] twice, p1, k2.
Round 20: K2, p2, k2, p3, [2/1 LPC, p1] twice, 2/1 LPC, k2.
Round 21: K2, p2, k8, p2, k2, p2, k4.
Round 22: K2, p2, k2, p4, [2/1 LPC, p1] twice, 2/1 LPC, k1.
Round 23: K2, p2, k9, p2, k2, p2, k3.
Round 24: K2, p2, k2, p5, [2/1 LPC, p1] twice, 2/1 LPC.

Soothingly simple lace rib means these Decca socks are perfect for knitting or wearing while snuggled up on the sofa.

Socks on the Decca!

Decca

YARN
John Arbon Textiles Exmoor Sock Yarn (85% Exmoor Blueface, 15% nylon; 400m [440yds] per 100g skein) 1 skein in Blossom

NEEDLES
2.5mm [UK 13-12/US 1-2] 80cm [32in] circular needles or DPNs (or size needed to get correct tension)
Stitch markers
Tapestry needle

TENSION
36 sts and 50 rounds = 10cm [4in] over st st
20 sts = 4.5cm [1¾in] over lace panel (unstretched)
24 rounds = 5cm [2in] over lace panel (unstretched)

SIZES
Small (Medium, Large)
To fit foot circumference: 20.5 (23, 25.5) cm [8 (9, 10) in]
Actual foot circumference of sock (unstretched): 17 (19, 22) cm [6¾ (7½, 8¾) in]
Length of leg to top of heel flap: 14.5cm [5¾in]
Foot length is fully adjustable within the pattern.
Finished sock measures 0.5cm [¼in] less than actual foot length, to ensure a good fit.

PATTERN NOTES
The charted stitch patterns are also given as written instructions at the end of the pattern.

ABBREVIATIONS
See full list of abbreviations on page 84.

The wonderful throw that Sigorni is nestled on was crocheted by Rachel's Mum, who improvised the pattern.

SOCK ONE

CUFF AND LEG

Cast on 64 (74, 84) sts. Join to work in the round, being careful not to twist. Place marker for start of round.

Round 1: *[K2, p1, k1tbl, p1] 2 (3, 4) times, k2, reading from right to left, work 20 sts from row 1 of chart A; rep from * once more.

Last round sets rib and chart A patterns. Working next row of chart A each time, continue as set until chart A has been completed 5 times (40 rounds).

Partial round: Remove start of round marker, k6 (9, 11), place marker for new start of round.

Round 41: K6 (8, 11), work 20 sts from row 1 of chart A, k12 (17, 22), work 20 sts from row 1 of chart A, k6 (9, 11).

Last round sets st st and chart A pattern. Continue to work in pattern as set, working next row of chart A each time, until chart A has been completed a further 4 times (32 rounds).

HEEL FLAP

Turn work so WS is facing. Heel flap will be worked back and forth on the next 32 (38, 42) beginning with a WS row. Keep remaining 32 (36, 42) sts on needles for instep.

Row 1 (WS): Sl1 wyif, p31 (37, 41).
Row 2 (RS): *Sl1 wyib, k1; rep from * to end.

Rep the last 2 rows a further 14 times then work row 1 once more.

HEEL TURN

Row 1 (RS): Sl1 wyib, k18 (20, 22), ssk, k1, turn, leaving remaining 10 (14, 16) sts unworked.
Row 2 (WS): Sl1 wyif, p7 (5, 5), p2tog, p1, turn, leaving remaining 10 (14, 16) sts unworked.
Row 3: Sl1 wyib, knit to 1 st before gap, ssk, k1, turn.
Row 4: Sl1 wyif, purl to 1 st before gap, p2tog, p1, turn.

Rep last 2 rows a further 4 (6, 7) times. All heel sts have been worked. 20 (22, 24) heel sts remain.

GUSSET

Begin working in the round again as follows:

Set-up round: Sl1 wyib, k19 (21, 23), pick up and knit 16 sts along edge of heel flap (1 st in each slipped st along edge of flap), work across 32 (36, 42) instep sts as follows: K6 (8, 11), work 20 sts from row 1 of chart A, k6 (8, 11), pick up and knit 16 sts along edge of heel flap, k36 (38, 40). Place marker for new start of round (at start of instep sts). 84 (90, 98) sts.

Round 1: K6 (8, 11), work 20 sts from next row of chart A, k6 (8, 11), ssk, knit to last 2 sts, k2tog. 2 sts dec.
Round 2: K6 (8, 11), work 20 sts from next row of chart A, k6 (8, 11), knit to end.

Working next row of chart each time, rep last 2 rounds a further 9 (8, 6) times. 20 (18, 14) sts dec; 64 (72, 84) sts.

Pattern continues on page 33.

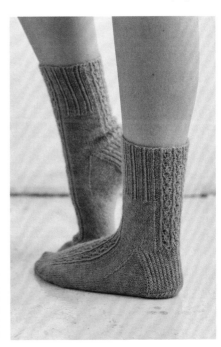

Decca

Charts

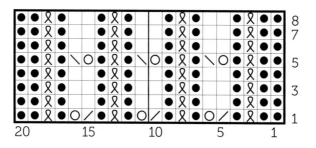

KEY

☐	knit
●	purl
⅄	k1tbl
╲	ssk
╱	k2tog
○	yarnover

CHART A

20		15		10		5		1	

Rows numbered on right: 8, 7, 5, 3, 1

WRITTEN CHART INSTRUCTIONS

CHART A

20 STS AND 8 ROUNDS

Round 1: P2, [k1tbl, p1, k2tog, yo, p1] 3 times, k1tbl, p2.

Rounds 2-4: P2, [k1tbl, p1, k2, p1] 3 times, k1tbl, p2.

Round 5: P2, [k1tbl, p1, yo, ssk, p1] 3 times, k1tbl, p2.

Rounds 6-8: Rep rounds 2-4.

Decca

Pattern continues:

You now have 32 (36, 42) sts each on instep and sole.

FOOT

Work as set (st st and chart A on instep and st st on sole) until the sock measures 5 (5.5, 6.5) cm [2 (2¼, 2½) in] less than the desired foot length.

TOE

Round 1: Knit.
Round 2: K1, ssk, k26 (30, 36), k2tog, k1, pm, k1, ssk, knit to last 3 sts, k2tog, k1. 60 (68, 80) sts.
Round 3: Knit.
Round 4: *K1, ssk, knit to 3 sts before marker, k2tog, k1, slm; rep from * once more. 4 sts dec.
Rep last 2 rounds a further 9 (10, 13) times. 40 (44, 56) sts dec; 20 (24, 24) sts remain.
Cut yarn, leaving a 30cm [12in] tail. Graft sts together using Kitchener stitch. Weave in ends.

SOCK TWO
CUFF AND LEG

Cast on 64 (74, 84) sts. Join to work in the round, being careful not to twist. Place marker for start of round.

Round 1: *[K2, p1, k1tbl, p1] 2 (3, 4) times, k2, work 20 sts from **row 5** of chart A; rep from * once more.
Last round sets rib and chart A patterns. Working next row of chart A each time, continue as set until row 4 of chart A has been completed 5 times (40 rounds).
Partial round: Remove start of round marker, k6 (9, 11), place marker for new start of round.
Round 41: K6 (8, 11), work 20 sts from **row 5** of chart A, k12 (17, 22), work 20 sts from row 5 of chart A, k6 (9, 11).
Last round sets st st and chart A pattern. Continue to work in pattern as set, working next row of chart A each time, until row 4 of chart A has been completed a further 4 times (32 rounds).

HEEL FLAP AND TURN, GUSSET, FOOT AND TOE

Work as Sock One.

The cables on these socks twist and turn like twisty-turny things - make sure you don't miss a trick!

Delbert

sock of ages!

Delbert

YARN
Green Version: Leading Men Fiber Arts, Spotlight (80% superwash Bluefaced Leicester wool, 20% nylon; 384m [400yds] per 100g skein) 1 skein in Dirty Truce
Purple Version: Whimsy Sokkusu O max (100% superwash merino; 495m [541yds] per 150g skein) 1 skein in Man of Rock

NEEDLES
2.5mm [UK 13-12/US 1-2] 80cm [32in] circular needles or DPNs (or size needed to get correct tension)
Cable needle
Stitch markers
Tapestry needle

TENSION
36 sts and 50 rounds = 10cm [4in] over st st
14 sts = 3cm [1¼in] over p2, 10 sts of cable pattern, p2
32 rounds = 5.5cm [2¼in] over cable pattern

SIZES
Small (Medium, Large)
To fit foot circumference: 20.5 (23, 25.5) cm [8 (9, 10) in]
Actual foot circumference of sock (unstretched): 16.5 (19, 21) cm [6½ (7½, 8¼) in]
Length of leg to top of heel flap: 14cm [5½in]
Foot length is fully adjustable within the pattern. Finished sock measures 0.5cm [¼in] less than actual foot length, to ensure a good fit.

PATTERN NOTES
The charted stitch patterns are also given as written instructions at the end of the pattern.

ABBREVIATIONS
2/2 LC: Slip next 2 sts to cable needle and place at front of work, k2, then k2 from cable needle
2/2 RC: Slip next 2 sts to cable needle and place at back of work, k2, then k2 from cable needle
2/2 LPC: Slip next 2 sts to cable needle and place at front of work, p2, then k2 from cable needle
2/2 RPC: Slip next 2 sts to cable needle and place at back of work, k2, then p2 from cable needle
See full list of abbreviations on page 84.

BOTH SOCKS

CUFF

Cast on 64 (72, 80) sts. Join to work in the round, being careful not to twist. Place marker for start of round.

Round 1: *K1 (2, 3), p2, [k2, p2] 3 times, k1 (2, 3); rep from * to end.
Round 2: *K1 (2, 3), p2, k10, p2, k1 (2, 3); rep from * to end.
Last 2 rounds set rib pattern. Rep rounds 1 and 2 a further 6 times (14 rounds).

LEG

Round 1: *K1 (2, 3), p2, reading from right to left, work 10 sts from row 1 of chart A, p2, k2 (4, 6), p2, reading from right to left, work 10 sts from row 1 of chart B, p2, k1 (2, 3); rep from * once more.
Last round sets rib and chart patterns. Working next row of charts each time, continue in pattern as set until charts have been completed twice (64 rounds).

HEEL FLAP

Turn work so WS is facing. Heel flap will be worked back and forth on the next 32 (36, 40) sts beginning with a WS row. Keep remaining 32 (36, 40) sts on needles for instep.

Row 1 (WS): Sl1 wyif, p0 (1, 2), k2, [p2, k2] 3 times, p2 (4, 6), k2, [p2, k2] 3 times, p1 (2, 3).
Row 2 (RS): *Sl1 wyib, k0 (1, 2), p2, k10, p2, k2 (4, 6), p2, k10, p2, k1 (2, 3).
Rep the last 2 rows a further 14 times then work row 1 once more.

HEEL TURN

Row 1 (RS): Sl1 wyib, k18 (20, 22), ssk, k1, turn, leaving remaining 10 (12, 14) sts unworked.
Row 2 (WS): Sl1 wyif, p7, p2tog, p1, turn, leaving remaining 10 (12, 14) sts unworked.
Row 3: Sl1 wyib, knit to 1 st before gap, ssk, k1, turn.
Row 4: Sl1 wyif, purl to 1 st before gap, p2tog, p1, turn.
Rep last 2 rows a further 4 (5, 6) times. All heel sts have been worked. 20 (22, 24) heel sts remain.

GUSSET

Begin working in the round again as follows:

Set-up round: Sl1 wyib, k19 (21, 23), pick up and knit 16 sts along edge of heel flap (1 st in each slipped st along edge of flap), work across 32 (36, 40) instep sts as follows: K1 (2, 3), p2, work row 1 of chart A, p2, k2 (4, 6), p2, work row 1 of chart B, p2, k1 (2, 3), pick up and knit 16 sts along edge of heel flap, k36 (38, 40). Place marker for new start of round (at start of instep sts). 84 (90, 96) sts.

Round 1: K1 (2, 3), p2, work row 2 of chart A, p2, k2 (4, 6), p2, work row 2 of chart B, p2, k1 (2, 3), ssk, knit to last 2 sts, k2tog. 2 sts dec.
Round 2: K1 (2, 3), p2, work row 3 of chart A, p2, k2 (4, 6), p2, work row 3 of chart B, p2, k1 (2, 3), knit to end.
Working next row of charts each time, rep last 2 rounds a further 9 (8, 7) times. 20 (18, 16) sts dec; 64 (72, 80) sts remain. You now have 32 (36, 40) sts each on instep and on sole.

Pattern continues on page 39.

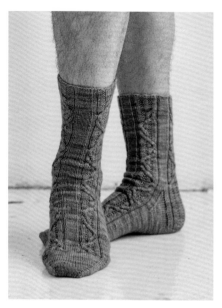
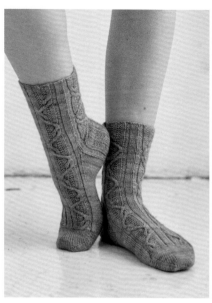
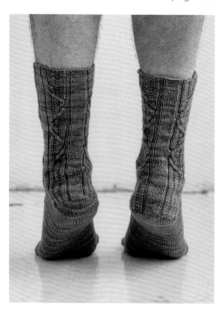

Delbert

Charts

KEY

☐ knit

⬤ purl

⬰ **2/2 LC:** Slip next 2 sts to cable needle and place at front of work, k2, then k2 from cable needle.

⬰ **2/2 RC:** Slip next 2 sts to cable needle and place at back of work, k2, then k2 from cable needle.

⬰ **2/2 LPC:** Slip next 2 sts to cable needle and place at front of work, p2, then k2 from cable needle.

⬰ **2/2 RPC:** Slip next 2 sts to cable needle and place at back of work, k2, then p2 from cable needle.

CHART B

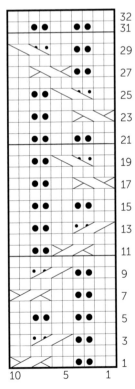

CHART A

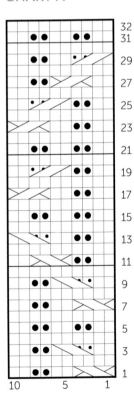

Delbert

Pattern continues:

FOOT

Work as set (rib and charts on instep and st st on sole) until the sock measures 5 (5.5, 6.5) cm [2 (2¼, 2½) in] less than the desired foot length.

TOE

Round 1: Knit.

Round 2: K1, ssk, k26 (30, 34), k2tog, k1, pm, k1, ssk, knit to last 3 sts, k2tog, k1. 60 (68, 76) sts.

Round 3: Knit.

Round 4: *K1, ssk, knit to 3 sts before marker, k2tog, k1, slm; rep from * once more. 4 sts dec.

Rep last 2 rounds a further 9 (10, 12) times. 40 (44, 52) sts dec; 20 (24, 24) sts remain.

Cut yarn, leaving a 30cm [12in] tail. Graft sts together using Kitchener stitch. Weave in ends.

WRITTEN CHART INSTRUCTIONS

CHART A

10 STS AND 32 ROUNDS

Round 1: 2/2 LC, k2, p2, k2.

Round 2 and all even-numbered rounds: Knit.

Round 3: K2, 2/2 LPC, p2, k2.

Round 5: [K2, p2] twice, k2.

Round 7: Rep round 1.

Round 9: Rep round 3.

Round 11: K2, p2, 2/2 LC, k2.

Round 13: K2, p2, k2, 2/2 LPC.

Round 15: Rep round 5.

Round 17: K2, p2, k2, 2/2 RC.

Round 19: K2, p2, 2/2 RPC, k2.

Round 21: Rep round 5.

Round 23: Rep round 17.

Round 25: Rep round 19.

Round 27: K2, 2/2 RC, p2, k2.

Round 29: 2/2 RPC, k2, p2, k2.

Round 31: Rep round 5.

Round 32: Rep round 2.

CHART B

10 STS AND 32 ROUNDS

Round 1: K2, p2, k2, 2/2 RC.

Round 2 and all even-numbered rounds: Knit.

Round 3: K2, p2, 2/2 RPC, k2.

Round 5: [K2, p2] twice, k2.

Round 7: Rep round 1.

Round 9: Rep round 3.

Round 11: K2, 2/2 RC, p2, k2.

Round 13: 2/2 RPC, k2, p2, k2.

Round 15: Rep round 5.

Round 17: 2/2 LC, k2, p2, k2.

Round 19: K2, 2/2 LPC, p2, k2.

Round 21: Rep round 5.

Round 23: Rep round 17.

Round 25: Rep round 19.

Round 27: K2, p2, 2/2 LC, k2.

Round 29: K2, p2, k2, 2/2 LPC.

Round 31: Rep round 5.

Round 32: Rep round 2.

Sidney
The Sock !

An offbeat, fraternal pair of socks - the graphic cable patterns are reversed on the second sock.

Sidney

YARN
Madelinetosh Tosh Sock (100% superwash merino; 384m [395yds] per 100g skein) 1 skein in Neon Peach

NEEDLES
2.5mm [UK 13-12/US 1-2] 80cm [32in] circular needles or DPNs (or size needed to get correct tension)
Cable needle
Stitch markers
Tapestry needle

TENSION
36 sts and 50 rounds = 10cm [4in] over st st
9 sts = 2cm [¾in] over chart A pattern
18 sts = 4.5cm [1¾in] over chart B pattern (2 repeats)

SIZES
Small (Medium, Large)
To fit foot circumference: 20.5 (23, 25.5) cm [8 (9, 10) in]
Actual foot circumference of sock (unstretched; average of Socks One and Two): 17 (19, 21) cm [6¾ (7½, 8¼) in]
Length of leg to top of heel flap: 14.5cm [5¾in]
Foot length is fully adjustable within the pattern. Finished sock measures 0.5cm [¼in] less than actual foot length, to ensure a good fit.

PATTERN NOTES
The charted stitch patterns are also given as written instructions at the end of the pattern. These socks are designed to be non-identical. If you would prefer identical socks, simply work two Sock Ones (or Twos). The two socks have very slightly different foot circumferences (by 0.5cm [¼in]) due to the different tensions of the two charted patterns.

ABBREVIATIONS

1/1 LT: Slip next st to cable needle and place at front of work, k1tbl, then k1tbl from cable needle

1/1 RT: Slip next st to cable needle and place at back of work, k1tbl, then k1tbl from cable needle

1/1 LPT: Slip next st to cable needle and place at front of work, p1, then k1tbl from cable needle

1/1 RPT: Slip next st to cable needle and place at back of work, k1tbl, then p1 from cable needle

2/1 LC: Slip next 2 sts to cable needle and place at front of work, k1, then k2 from cable needle

2/1 RC: Slip next st to cable needle and place at back of work, k2, then k1 from cable needle

2/1/2 LPC: Slip next 3 sts to cable needle and place at front of work, k2, move last st from cable needle back on to left needle, p this st, k2 from cable needle

2/1/2 RPC: Slip next 3 sts to cable needle and place at back of work, k2, move last st from cable needle back on to left needle, p this st, k2 from cable needle

See full list of abbreviations on page 84.

SOCK ONE

CUFF AND LEG

Cast on 66 (72, 78) sts. Join to work in the round, being careful not to twist. Place marker for start of round.

Round 1: *P2 (3, 4), reading from right to left, work 9 sts from row 1 of chart A, p2 (3, 4), reading from right to left, work 9 sts from row 1 of chart B; rep from * to end. Last round sets reverse st st and chart patterns. Working next row of charts each time, continue in pattern as set until charts have been completed 4 times and rounds 1-8 have been worked once more (72 rounds).

Heel set-up (partial round): Remove marker, p1.

HEEL FLAP

Turn work so WS is facing. Heel flap will be worked back and forth on the next 33 (35, 37) sts beginning with a WS row. Keep remaining 33 (37, 41) sts on needles for instep.

Row 1 (WS): Sl1 wyif, p32 (34, 36).
Row 2 (RS): *Sl1 wyib, k1; rep from * to last st, k1.

Rep the last 2 rows a further 14 times then work row 1 once more.

HEEL TURN

Row 1 (RS): Sl1 wyib, k17 (19, 19), ssk, k1, turn, leaving remaining 12 (12, 14) sts unworked.
Row 2 (WS): Sl1 wyif, p4 (6, 4), p2tog, p1, turn, leaving remaining 12 (12, 14) sts unworked.
Row 3: Sl1 wyib, knit to 1 st before gap, ssk, k1, turn.
Row 4: Sl1 wyif, purl to 1 st before gap, p2tog, p1, turn.
Rep last 2 rows a further 5 (5, 6) times. All heel sts have been worked. 19 (21, 21) heel sts remain.

GUSSET

Begin working in the round again as follows:

Set-up round: Sl1 wyib, k18 (20, 20), pick up and knit 16 sts along edge of heel flap (1 st in each slipped st along edge of flap), work across 33 (37, 41) instep sts as foll: P1 (2, 3), work row 9 of chart A, p2 (3, 4), work row 9 of chart B, p2 (3, 4), work row 9 of chart A, p1 (2, 3), pick up and knit 16 sts along edge of heel flap, k35 (37, 37).

Pattern continues on page 44.

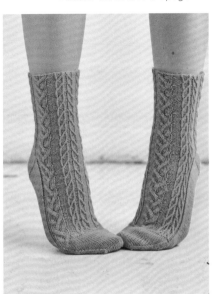

Sidney

Charts

KEY

- ☐ knit
- ● purl
- ⊗ k1tbl
- **1/1 LT:** Slip next st to cable needle and place at front of work, k1tbl, then k1tbl from cable needle.
- **1/1 RT:** Slip next st to cable needle and place at back of work, k1tbl, then k1tbl from cable needle.
- **1/1 LPT:** Slip next st to cable needle and place at front of work, p1, then k1tbl from cable needle.
- **1/1 RPT:** Slip next st to cable needle and place at back of work, k1tbl, then p1 from cable needle.
- **2/1 LC:** Slip next 2 sts to cable needle and place at front of work, k1, then k2 from cable needle.
- **2/1 RC:** Slip next st to cable needle and place at back of work, k2, then k1 from cable needle.
- **2/1/2 LPC:** Slip next 3 sts to cable needle and place at front of work, k2, move last st from cable needle back on to left needle, p this st, k2 from cable needle.
- **2/1/2 RPC:** Slip next 3 sts to cable needle and place at back of work, k2, move last st from cable needle back on to left needle, p this st, k2 from cable needle.

CHART B

CHART A

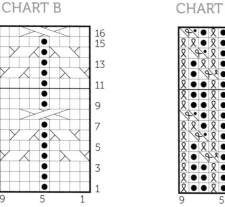

Pattern continues:

Place marker for new start of round (at start of instep sts). 84 (90, 94) sts.

Round 1: P1 (2, 3), work row 10 of chart A, p2 (3, 4), work row 10 of chart B, p2 (3, 4), work row 10 of chart A, p1 (2, 3), ssk, knit to last 2 sts, k2tog. 2 sts dec.

Round 2: P1 (2, 3), work row 11 of chart A, p2 (3, 4), work row 11 of chart B, p2 (3, 4), work row 11 of chart A, p1 (2, 3), knit to end.

Working next row of charts each time, rep last 2 rounds a further 8 (8, 6) times. 18 (18, 14) sts dec; 66 (72, 80) sts remain. You now have 33 (37, 41) sts on instep and 33 (35, 39) sts on sole.

FOOT

Work as set (reverse st st and charts on instep and st st on sole) until the sock measures 5.5 (5.5, 6.5) cm (2¼ (2¼, 2½) in) less than the desired foot length.

MEDIUM AND LARGE SIZES ONLY

Toe set-up round: K1, ssk, k- (31, 35), k2tog, knit to end. - (2, 2) sts dec; - (70, 78) sts remain.

TOE

ALL SIZES

Round 1: Knit.
Round 2: K1, ssk, k27 (29, 33), k2tog, k1, pm, k1, ssk, knit to last 3 sts, k2tog, k1. 62 (66, 74) sts.
Round 3: Knit.
Round 4: *K1, ssk, knit to 3 sts before marker, k2tog, k1, slm; rep from * once more. 4 sts dec.
Rep last 2 rounds a further 10 (10, 12) times. 44 (44, 52) sts dec; 18 (22, 22) sts remain.
Cut yarn, leaving a 30cm [12in] tail. Graft sts together using Kitchener stitch. Weave in ends.

SOCK TWO

CUFF AND LEG

Cast on 66 (72, 78) sts. Join to work in the round, being careful not to twist. Place marker for start of round.
Round 1: *P2 (3, 4), work 9 sts from **row 9** of chart B, p2 (3, 4), work 9 sts from **row 9** of chart A; rep from * to end.
Last round sets reverse st st and chart patterns. Working next row of charts each time, continue in pattern as set until rounds 9-16 of charts have been completed, then rounds 1-16 worked a further 4 times (72 rounds).
Heel set-up (partial round): Remove marker, p1.

HEEL FLAP AND TURN

Work as Sock One.

GUSSET

Begin working in the round again as follows:
Set-up round: Sl1 wyib, k18 (20, 20), pick up and knit 16 sts along edge of heel flap (1 st in each slipped st along edge of flap), work across 33 (37, 41) instep sts as follows: P1 (2, 3), work row 1 of chart B, p2 (3, 4), work row 1 of chart A, p2 (3, 4), work row 1 of chart B, p1 (2, 3), pick up and knit 16 sts along edge of heel flap, k35 (37, 37).
Place marker for new start of round (at start of instep sts). 84 (90, 94) sts.

Round 1: P1 (2, 3), work row 2 of chart B, p2 (3, 4), work row 2 of chart A, p2 (3, 4), work row 2 of chart B, p1 (2, 3), ssk, knit to last 2 sts, k2tog. 2 sts dec.
Round 2: P1 (2, 3), work row 3 of chart B, p2 (3, 4), work row 3 of chart A, p2 (3, 4), work row 3 of chart B, p1 (2, 3), knit to end.
Working next row of charts each time, rep last 2 rounds a further 8 (8, 6) times. 18 (18, 14) sts dec; 66 (72, 80) sts.
You now have 33 (37, 41) sts on instep and 33 (35, 39) sts on sole.

FOOT AND TOE
Work as Sock One.

WRITTEN CHART INSTRUCTIONS

CHART A
9 STS AND 16 ROUNDS
Rounds 1-3: K1tbl, p2, k1tbl, p1, k1tbl, p2, k1tbl.
Round 4: K1tbl, p1, 1/1 RT, p1, 1/1 LT, p1, k1tbl.
Round 5: K1tbl, [p1, k2tbl] twice, p1, k1tbl.
Round 6: K1tbl, 1/1 RPT, k1tbl, p1, k1tbl, 1/1 LPT, k1tbl.
Round 7: K2tbl, [p1, k1tbl] twice, p1, k2tbl.
Round 8: 1/1 RPT, [p1, k1tbl] twice, p1, 1/1 LPT.
Rounds 9-16: Rep rounds 1-8.

CHART B
9 STS AND 16 ROUNDS
Round 1 and all odd-numbered rounds: K4, p1, k4.
Round 2: K4, p1, k4.
Round 4: 2/1 LC, k1, p1, k1, 2/1 RC.
Round 6: K1, 2/1 LC, p1, 2/1 RC, k1.
Round 8: K2, 2/1/2 RPC, k2.
Round 10: K4, p1, k4.
Round 12: Rep round 4.
Round 14: Rep round 6.
Round 16: K2, 2/1/2 LPC, k2.

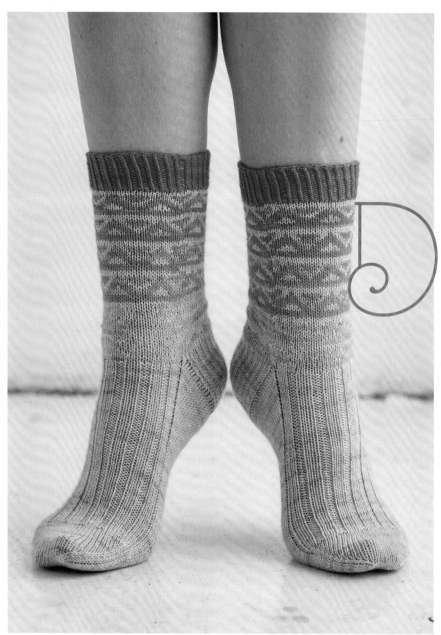

Designed for a chromatic set of mini-skeins, this rhythmic colourwork pattern will help your socks fly off the needles.

Otis
born to sock!

Otis

YARN

The Knitting Goddess Merino Nylon Sock Yarn (75% superwash merino, 25% nylon; 380m [415 yds] per 115g skein)

MC: 1 x 115g skein in Biscuit

The Knitting Goddess Merino Nylon Sock Yarn (75% superwash merino, 25% nylon; 40m [43yds] per 10g mini skeins)

CC1-7: 1 set of 7 mini skeins in Shades of Orange (where CC1 is the darkest shade and CC7 is the palest shade)

NEEDLES

2.5mm [UK 13-12/US 1-2] 80cm [32in] circular needles or DPNs (or size needed to get correct tension)
Stitch markers
Tapestry needle

TENSION

36 sts and 50 rounds = 10cm [4in] over st st
16 rounds = 3cm [1¼in] over twisted rib cuff
38 sts and 45 rounds = 10cm [4in] over stranded colourwork pattern
46 sts and 50 rounds = 10cm [4in] over rib pattern (unstretched)

SIZES

Small (Medium, Large)
To fit foot circumference: 20.5 (23, 25.5) cm [8 (9, 10) in]
Actual foot circumference of sock (unstretched): 15 (18, 20.5) cm [6 (7, 8) in]
Length of leg to top of heel flap: 16.5cm [6½in]
Foot length is fully adjustable within the pattern.
Finished sock measures 0.5cm [¼in] less than actual foot length, to ensure a good fit.

ABBREVIATIONS

MC: Main colour
CC: Contrast colour
See full list of abbreviations on page 84.

SOCK ONE

CUFF

With CC1, cast on 60 (70, 80) sts. Join to work in the round, being careful not to twist. Place marker for start of round.

Round 1: *K1 tbl, p1; rep from * to end. Work this round a further 15 times (16 rounds). Break yarn.

LEG

Join in MC.
Round 1: Reading from right to left, [work 10 sts from row 1 of chart A] 6 (7, 8) times. When required, join in CC2 and use a stranded knitting technique where MC and CC are used on the same row. Working next row of chart A each time, continue in pattern as set until chart A has been completed.
Work chart A a further 5 times, changing CC for the next mini skein in the sequence each time, thus ending with MC and CC7 (60 rounds).

Remaining sock is worked in MC only.

HEEL FLAP

Turn work so WS is facing. Heel flap will be worked back and forth on the next 30 (35, 40) sts, beginning with a WS row. Keep remaining 30 (35, 40) sts on needles for instep.

Row 1 (WS): Sl1 wyif, p29 (34, 39).
Row 2 (RS): *Sl1 wyib, k1; rep from * to last 0 (1, 0) st, k0 (1, 0).
Rep these 2 rows a further 14 times, then work row 1 once more.

HEEL TURN

Row 1 (RS): Sl1 wyib, k16 (19, 22), ssk, k1, turn, leaving remaining 10 (12, 14) sts unworked.
Row 2 (WS): Sl1 wyif, p5 (6, 7), p2tog, p1, turn, leaving remaining 10 (12, 14) sts unworked.
Row 3: Sl1 wyib, knit to 1 st before gap, ssk, k1, turn.
Row 4: Sl1 wyif, purl to 1 st before gap,

p2tog, p1, turn.
Rep last 2 rows 4 (5, 6) more times. All heel sts have been worked. 18 (21, 24) heel sts remain.

GUSSET

Begin working in the round again as follows:
Set-up round: Sl1 wyib, k17 (20, 23), pick up and knit 16 sts along edge of heel flap (1 st in each slipped st along edge of flap), k30 (35, 40) instep sts, pick up and knit 16 sts along edge of heel flap, k34 (37, 40). Place marker for new start of round (at start of instep sts). 80 (88, 96) sts.

Round 1: [P1, k3, p1] 6 (7, 8) times, ssk, knit to last 2 sts, k2tog. 2 sts dec.
Round 2: [P1, k3, p1] 6 (7, 8) times, knit to end.
Rep last 2 rounds a further 9 (8, 7) times. 20 (18, 16) sts dec; 60 (70, 80) sts remain. You now have 30 (35, 40) sts each on instep and sole.

FOOT

Work as set (rib on instep and st st on sole) until the sock measures 4.5 (5.5, 6.5) cm [1¾ (2¼, 2½) in] less than the desired foot length.

TOE

Round 1: Knit.
Round 2: K1, ssk, k24 (29, 34), k2tog, k1, pm, k1, ssk, knit to last 3 sts, k2tog, k1. 56 (66, 76) sts.
Round 3: Knit.
Round 4: *K1, ssk, knit to 3 sts before marker, k2tog, k1, slm; rep from * once more. 4 sts dec.
Rep last 2 rounds a further 8 (10, 12) times. 36 (44, 52) sts dec; 20 (22, 24) sts remain.

Cut yarn, leaving a 30cm [12in] tail. Graft sts together using Kitchener stitch. Weave in ends.

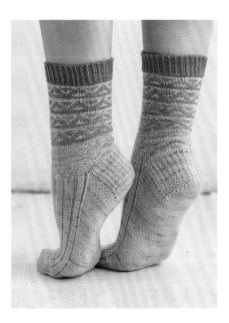

KEY

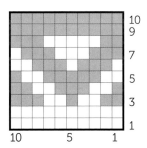

☐ knit using MC

▨ knit using CC as indicated in written instructions

CHART A

										10
										9
										7
										5
										3
										1

10   5   1

SOCK TWO

CUFF AND LEG

Work as Sock One.

HEEL SET-UP

Partial round: Using MC, k30 (35, 40). This marks the new start of the round, and ensures that the colourwork jog at the change of round is located on the inside of the ankle.

HEEL FLAP AND TURN, GUSSET, FOOT AND TOE

Work as Sock One.

averne works in a sweet shop, filling paper bags with sherbet pips and the other old-fashioned sweeties that inspired these socks.

Laverne a∂ngel of socks

Laverne

SIZES

Small (Medium, Large)
To fit foot circumference: 20.5 (23, 25.5) cm [8 (9, 10) in]
Actual foot circumference of sock (unstretched): 14.5 (18, 20.5) cm [5¾ (7, 8) in]
Length of leg to top of heel flap: 16.5cm [6½in]
Foot length is fully adjustable within the pattern.
Finished sock measures 0.5cm [¼in] less than actual foot length, to ensure a good fit.

PATTERN NOTES

The charted stitch patterns are also given as written instructions at the end of the pattern. Sock Two is worked in the same way as Sock One, simply substituting 1/1/1 LPT for the 1/1/1 RPT shown on the charts. This creates a mirrored second sock.

ABBREVIATIONS

3 st loop: Insert right needle into third st on left needle and draw this st over first 2 sts on left needle, and off the needle; k1, yo, k1.

1/1 LT: Slip next st to cable needle and place at front of work, k1tbl, then k1tbl from cable needle

1/1 RT: Slip next st to cable needle and place at back of work, k1tbl, then k1tbl from cable needle

1/1 LKT: Slip next st to cable needle and place at front of work, k1, then k1tbl from cable needle

1/1 RKT: Slip next st to cable needle and place at back of work, k1tbl, then k1 from cable needle

1/1 LPT: Slip next st to cable needle and place at front of work, p1, then k1tbl from cable needle

1/1 RPT: Slip next st to cable needle and place at back of work, k1tbl, then p1 from cable needle

1/1/1 LPT: Slip next 2 sts to cable needle and place at front of work, k1tbl, move last st from cable needle back on to left needle, p this st, k1tbl from cable needle

1/1/1 RPT: Slip next 2 sts to cable needle and place at back of work, k1tbl, move last st from cable needle back on to left needle, p this st, k1tbl from cable needle

See full list of abbreviations on page 84.

YARN

The Knitting Goddess Britsock Yarn (40% Bluefaced Leicester wool, 20% Wensleydale wool, 20% alpaca, 20% nylon; 400m [440yds] per 100g skein) 1 skein in Tangerine Sorbet

NEEDLES

2.5mm [UK 13-12/US 1-2] 80cm [32in] circular needles or DPNs (or size needed to get correct tension)
Stitch markers
Tapestry needle
Cable needle

TENSION

36 sts and 50 rounds = 10cm [4in] over st st
37 sts = 7.5cm [3in] over chart B, C or D cable pattern
24 rounds = 5cm [2in] over charted cable patterns

SOCK ONE

CUFF

Cast on 60 (72, 84) sts. Join to work in the round, being careful not to twist. Place marker for start of round.

Round 1: *P3, k1tbl, p1, k1tbl, p3, k3; rep from * to end.
Last round sets rib pattern, work this round a further 15 times (16 rounds).

LEG

Round 1: Reading from right to left, [work 12 sts from row 1 of chart A] 5 (6, 7) times.
Last round sets chart A pattern. Working next row of chart A each time, continue as set until chart A has been completed 5 times and round 1 has been worked once more (61 rounds).

SMALL AND LARGE SIZES

Partial round: Remove start of round marker, p1.

MEDIUM SIZE ONLY

Partial round: Remove start of round marker, p3, k1tbl, p1, k1tbl, p3, k1.

ALL SIZES

The partial round ensures that the heel flap is correctly positioned.

HEEL FLAP

Turn work so WS is facing. Heel flap will be worked back and forth on the next 29 (35, 41) beginning with a WS row. Keep remaining 31 (37, 43) sts on needles for instep.
Row 1 (WS): Sl1 wyif, p28 (34, 40).
Row 2 (RS): *Sl1 wyib, k1; rep from * to last st, k1.
Rep the last 2 rows a further 14 times then work row 1 once more.

HEEL TURN

Row 1 (RS): Sl1 wyib, k15 (19, 21), ssk, k1, turn, leaving remaining 10 (12, 16) sts unworked.
Row 2 (WS): Sl1 wyif, p4 (6, 4), p2tog, p1, turn, leaving remaining 10 (12, 16) sts unworked.
Row 3: Sl1 wyib, knit to 1 st before gap, ssk, k1, turn.

Row 4: Sl1 wyif, purl to 1 st before gap, p2tog, p1, turn.
Rep last 2 rows a further 4 (5, 7) times. All heel sts have been worked. 17 (21, 23) heel sts remain.

GUSSET

Begin working in the round again as follows:
Set-up round: Sl1 wyib, k16 (20, 22), pick up and knit 16 sts along edge of heel flap (1 st in each slipped st along edge of flap), work across 31 (37, 43) instep sts from row 1 of chart B (C, D), pick up and knit 16 sts along edge of heel flap, k33 (37, 39). Place marker for new start of round (at start of instep sts). 80 (90, 98) sts.

Round 1: Work 31 (37, 43) sts from row 2 of chart B (C, D), ssk, knit to last 2 sts, k2tog. 2 sts dec.
Round 2: Work 31 (37, 43) sts from row 3 of chart B (C, D), knit to end.
Working next row of chart each time, rep last 2 rounds a further 9 (8, 6) times. 20 (18, 14) sts dec; 60 (72, 84) sts.

You now have 31 (37, 43) sts on instep and 29 (35, 41) sts on sole.

FOOT

When row 24 of chart is complete, rep rows 5-24 only, working as set (chart B (C, D) on instep and st st on sole) until the sock measures 5 (5.5, 7) cm [2 (2¼, 2¾) in] less than the desired foot length.

Toe set-up round: K1, ssk, k25 (31, 37), k2tog, knit to end. 2 sts dec; 58 (70, 82) sts remain.

TOE

Round 1: Knit.
Round 2: K1, ssk, k23 (29, 35), k2tog, k1, pm, k1, ssk, knit to last 3 sts, k2tog, k1. 54 (66, 78) sts.
Round 3: Knit.
Round 4: *K1, ssk, knit to 3 sts before marker, k2tog, k1, slm; rep from * once more. 4 sts dec.
Rep last 2 rounds a further 8 (10, 13) times. 36 (44, 56) sts dec; 18 (22, 22) sts remain.
Cut yarn, leaving a 30cm [12in] tail. Graft sts together using Kitchener stitch. Weave in ends.

SOCK TWO

Work as Sock One, simply substituting 1/1/1 LPT for the 1/1/1 RPT shown on the charts and written instructions.

Laverne

Charts

KEY

☐ knit

● purl

X k1tbl

⧄ **1/1 LT:** Slip next st to cable needle and place at front of work, k1tbl, then k1tbl from cable needle.

⧄ **1/1 RT:** Slip next st to cable needle and place at back of work, k1tbl, then k1tbl from cable needle.

⧄ **1/1 LKT:** Slip next st to cable needle and place at front of work, k1, then k1tbl from cable needle.

⧄ **1/1 RKT:** Slip next st to cable needle and place at back of work, k1tbl, then k1 from cable needle.

⧄ **1/1 LPT:** Slip next st to cable needle and place at front of work, p1, then k1tbl from cable needle.

⧄ **1/1 RPT:** Slip next st to cable needle and place at back of work, k1tbl, then p1 from cable needle.

⧄ **1/1/1 RPT (Sock 1):** Slip next 2 sts to cable needle and place at back of work, k1tbl, move last st from cable needle back on to left needle, p this st, k1tbl from cable needle.

⧄ **1/1/1 LPT (Sock 2):** Slip next 2 sts to cable needle and place at front of work, k1tbl, move last st from cable needle back on to left needle, p this st, k1tbl from cable needle.

◁◌▷ **3 st loop:** Insert right needle into third st on left needle and draw this st over first 2 sts on left needle, and off the needle; k1, yo, k1.

☐ Pattern repeat

CHART D

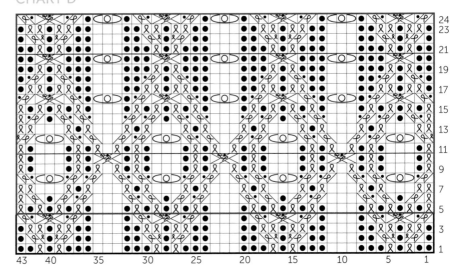

CHART C

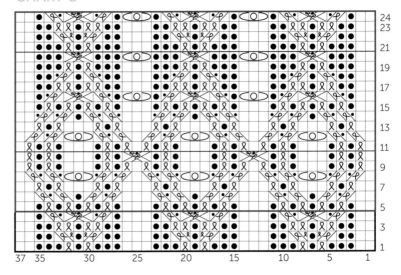

CHART B

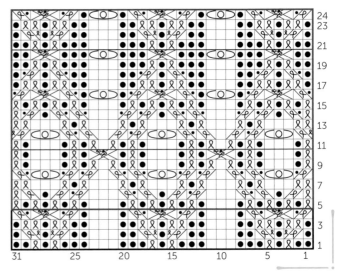

CHART A

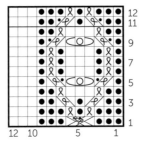

WRITTEN CHART INSTRUCTIONS

NOTE: When working Sock Two replace 1/1/1 RPT with 1/1/1 LPT throughout.

CHART A

12 STS AND 12 ROUNDS

Round 1: P3, 1/1/1 RPT, p3, k3.
Round 2: P3, k1tbl, p1, k1tbl, p3, k3.
Round 3: P2, 1/1 RKT, p1, 1/1 LKT, p2, k3.
Round 4: P2, k1tbl, k3, k1tbl, p2, k3.
Round 5: P1, 1/1 RPT, 3 st loop, 1/1 LPT, p1, k3.
Rounds 6-8: [P1, k1tbl, p1, k3] twice.
Round 9: P1, 1/1 LPT, 3 st loop, 1/1 RPT, p1, k3.
Round 10: Rep round 4.
Round 11: P2, 1/1 LPT, p1, 1/1 RPT, p2, k3.
Round 12: Rep round 2.

CHART B

31 STS AND 24 ROUNDS

Round 1: P2, [k1tbl, p1, k1tbl, p3, k3, p3] twice, k1tbl, p1, k1tbl, p2.
Round 2: P1, [1/1 RT, p1, 1/1 LT, p2, k3, p2] twice, 1/1 RT, p1, 1/1 LT, p1.
Round 3: P1, [k2tbl, p1, k2tbl, p2, k3, p2] twice, [k2tbl, p1] twice.
Round 4: [1/1 RPT, 1/1/1 RPT, 1/1 LPT, p1, k3, p1] twice, 1/1 RPT, 1/1/1 RPT, 1/1 LPT.
Round 5: *[K1tbl, p1] 4 times, k3, p1; rep from * once more, [k1tbl, p1] 3 times, k1tbl.
Round 6: K1tbl, [1/1 RKT, p1, 1/1 LKT, 1/1 LPT, k3, 1/1 RPT] twice, 1/1 RKT, p1, 1/1 LKT, k1tbl.
Round 7: K2tbl, [k3, k1tbl, p1, k1tbl] 4 times, k3, k2tbl.
Round 8: 1/1 RPT, [3 st loop, 1/1 LPT twice, k1, 1/1 RPT twice] twice, 3 st loop, 1/1 LPT.
Round 9: *K1tbl, p1, k3, [p1, k1tbl] twice, k1, k1tbl, p1: rep from * once more, k1tbl, p1, k3, p1, k1tbl.
Round 10: [K1tbl, p1, k3, p1, k1tbl, p1, 1/1/1 RPT, p1] twice, k1tbl, p1, k3, p1, k1tbl.
Round 11: Rep round 9.
Round 12: 1/1 LT, 3 st loop, 1/1 RPT, 1/1 RKT, k1, 1/1 LKT, 1/1 LPT, 3 st loop, 1/1 RPT, 1/1 RKT, k1, 1/1 LKT, 1/1 LPT, 3 st loop, 1/1 RT.
Round 13: Rep round 7.
Round 14: K1tbl, 1/1 LPT, p1, *[1/1 RPT] twice, k3, [1/1 LPT] twice, p1; rep from * once more, 1/1 RPT, k1tbl.
Round 15: Rep round 5.
Round 16: [1/1 LPT, 1/1/1 RPT, 1/1 RPT, p1, 3 st loop, p1] twice, 1/1 LPT, 1/1/1 RPT, 1/1 RPT.
Round 17: Rep round 3.
Round 18: P1, [1/1 LPT, p1, 1/1 RPT, p2, k3, p2] twice, 1/1 LPT, p1, 1/1 RPT, p1.

Round 19: Rep round 1.
Round 20: P2, [1/1/1 RPT, p3, 3 st loop, p3] twice, 1/1/1 RPT, p2.
Round 21: Rep round 1.
Round 22: Rep round 2.
Round 23: Rep round 3.
Round 24: [1/1 RPT, 1/1/1 RPT, 1/1 LPT, p1, 3 st loop, p1] twice, 1/1 RPT, 1/1/1 RPT, 1/1 LPT.
Rep rounds 5-24 only.

CHART C

37 STS AND 24 ROUNDS

Round 1: K2, [p3, k1tbl, p1, k1tbl, p3, k3] twice, p3, k1tbl, p1, k1tbl, p3, k2.
Round 2: K2, [p2, 1/1 RT, p1, 1/1 LT, p2, k3] twice, p2, 1/1 RT, p1, 1/1 LT, p2, k2.
Round 3: K2, [p2, k2tbl, p1, k2tbl, p2, k3] twice, p2, k2tbl, p1, k2tbl, p2, k2.
Round 4: K2, [p1, 1/1 RPT, 1/1/1 RPT, 1/1 LPT, p1, k3] twice, p1, 1/1 RPT, 1/1/1 RPT, 1/1 LPT, p1, k2.
Round 5: K2, *[p1, k1tbl] 4 times, p1, k3; rep from * once more, [p1, k1tbl] 4 times, p1, k2.
Round 6: K2, [1/1 RPT, 1/1 RKT, p1, 1/1 LKT, 1/1 LPT, k3] twice, 1/1 RPT, 1/1 RKT, p1, 1/1 LKT, 1/1 LPT, k2.
Round 7: K2, [k1tbl, p1, k1tbl, k3] 5 times, k1tbl, p1, k1tbl, k2.
Round 8: [K1, 1/1 RPT twice, 3 st loop, 1/1 LPT twice] 3 times, k1.
Round 9: *K1, [k1tbl, p1] twice, k3, [p1, k1tbl] twice; rep from * a further 2 times, k1.
Round 10: K1, k1tbl, [p1, k1tbl, p1, k3, p1, k1tbl, p1, 1/1/1 RPT] twice, p1, k1tbl, p1, k3, p1, k1tbl] twice, k1.
Round 11: Rep round 9.
Round 12: [K1, 1/1 LKT, 1/1 LPT, 3 st loop, 1/1 RPT, 1/1 RKT] 3 times, k1.
Round 13: Rep round 7.
Round 14: K2, *[1/1 LPT] twice, p1, [1/1 RPT] twice, k3; rep from * once more, [1/1 LPT] twice, p1, [1/1 RPT] twice, k2.
Round 15: Rep round 5.
Round 16: K2, [p1, 1/1 LPT, 1/1/1 RPT, 1/1 RPT, p1, 3 st loop] twice, p1, 1/1 LPT, 1/1/1 RPT, 1/1 RPT, p1, k2.
Round 17: Rep round 3.
Round 18: K2, [p2, 1/1 LPT, p1, 1/1 RPT, p2, k3] twice, p2, 1/1 LPT, p1, 1/1 RPT, p2, k2.
Round 19: Rep round 1.
Round 20: K2, [p3, 1/1/1 RPT, p3, 3 st loop] twice, p3, 1/1/1 RPT, p3, k2.
Round 21: Rep round 1.

Round 22: Rep round 2.
Round 23: Rep round 3.
Round 24: K2, [p1, 1/1 RPT, 1/1/1 RPT, 1/1 LPT, p1, 3 st loop] twice, p1, 1/1 RPT, 1/1/1 RPT, 1/1 LPT, p1, k2.
Rep rounds 5-24 only.

CHART D

43 STS AND 24 ROUNDS

Round 1: P2, [k1tbl, p1, k1tbl, p3, k3, p3] 3 times, k1tbl, p1, k1tbl, p2.
Round 2: P1, [1/1 RT, p1, 1/1 LT, p2, k3, p2] 3 times, 1/1 RT, p1, 1/1 LT, p1.
Round 3: P1, [k2tbl, p1, k2tbl, p2, k3, p2] 3 times, [k2tbl, p1] twice.
Round 4: [1/1 RPT, 1/1/1 RPT, 1/1 LPT, p1, k3, p1] 3 times, 1/1 RPT, 1/1/1 RPT, 1/1 LPT.
Round 5: *[K1tbl, p1] 4 times, k3, p1; rep from * a further 2 times, [k1tbl, p1] 3 times, k1tbl.
Round 6: K1tbl, [1/1 RKT, p1, 1/1 LKT, 1/1 LPT, k3, 1/1 RPT] 3 times, 1/1 RKT, p1, 1/1 LKT, k1tbl.
Round 7: K2tbl, [k3, k1tbl, p1, k1tbl] 6 times, k3, k2tbl.
Round 8: 1/1 RPT, [3 st loop, 1/1 LPT twice, k1, 1/1 RPT twice] 3 times, 3 st loop, 1/1 LPT.
Round 9: *K1tbl, p1, k3, [p1, k1tbl] twice, k1, k1tbl, p1; rep from * a further 2 times, k1tbl, p1, k3, p1, k1tbl.
Round 10: [K1tbl, p1, k3, p1, k1tbl, p1, 1/1/1 RPT, p1] 3 times, k1tbl, p1, k3, p1, k1tbl.
Round 11: Rep round 9.
Round 12: 1/1 LT, 3 st loop, 1/1 RPT, 1/1 RKT, [k1, 1/1 LKT, 1/1 LPT, 3 st loop, 1/1 RPT, 1/1 RKT] twice, k1, 1/1 LKT, 1/1 LPT, 3 st loop, 1/1 RT.
Round 13: Rep round 7.
Round 14: K1tbl, 1/1 LPT, *p1, [1/1 RPT] twice, k3, [1/1 LPT] twice; rep from * a further 2 times, p1, 1/1 RPT, k1tbl.
Round 15: Rep round 5.
Round 16: [1/1 LPT, 1/1/1 RPT, 1/1 RPT, p1, 3 st loop, p1] 3 times, 1/1 LPT, 1/1/1 RPT, 1/1 RPT.
Round 17: Rep round 3.
Round 18: P1, [1/1 LPT, p1, 1/1 RPT, p2, k3, p2] 3 times, 1/1 LPT, p1, 1/1 RPT, p1.
Round 19: Rep round 1.
Round 20: P2, [1/1/1 RPT, p3, 3 st loop, p3] 3 times, 1/1/1 RPT, p2.
Round 21: Rep round 1.
Round 22: Rep round 2.
Round 23: Rep round 3.
Round 24: [1/1 RPT, 1/1/1 RPT, 1/1 LPT, p1, 3 st loop, p1] 3 times, 1/1 RPT, 1/1/1 RPT, 1/1 LPT.
Rep rounds 5-24 only.

Intricate cables and travelling twisted stitch motifs are balanced by a simple broken twisted rib pattern that flows down the socks.

my sock love

Eula

Eula

YARN:
Blue Moon Fiber Arts, Socks That Rock Lightweight (100% Superwash Merino; 370m [405yds] per 148g skein) 1 skein in Vancouver Violet

NEEDLES
2.5mm [UK 13-12/US 1-2] 80cm [32in] circular needles or DPNs (or size needed to get correct tension)
Stitch markers
Tapestry needle
Cable needle

TENSION
36 sts and 50 rounds = 10cm [4in] over st st
23 sts = 5.5cm [2¼in] over chart A or B cable pattern
40 sts and 48 rounds = 10cm [4in] over broken twisted rib pattern

SIZES
Small (Medium, Large)
To fit foot circumference: 20.5 (23, 25.5) cm [8 (9, 10) in]
Actual foot circumference of sock (unstretched): 17 (19.5. 22) cm [6¾ (7¾, 8¾) in]
Length of leg to top of heel flap: 15cm [6in]
Foot length is fully adjustable within the pattern.
Finished sock measures 0.5cm [¼in] less than actual foot length, to ensure a good fit.

PATTERN NOTES
The charted stitch patterns are also given as written instructions at the end of the pattern.

ABBREVIATIONS

1/1 LC: Slip next st to cable needle and place at front of work, k1, then k1 from cable needle

1/1 RC: Slip next st to cable needle and place at back of work, k1, then k1 from cable needle

1/1 LT: Slip next st to cable needle and place at front of work, k1tbl, then k1tbl from cable needle

1/1 RT: Slip next st to cable needle and place at back of work, k1tbl, then k1tbl from cable needle

1/1 LKT: Slip next st to cable needle and place at front of work, k1, then k1tbl from cable needle

1/1 RKT: Slip next st to cable needle and place at back of work, k1tbl, then k1 from cable needle

1/1 LPT: Slip next st to cable needle and place at front of work, p1, then k1tbl from cable needle

1/1 RPT: Slip next st to cable needle and place at back of work, k1tbl, then p1 from cable needle

2/2 LKT: Slip next 2 sts to cable needle and place at front of work, k2, then k2tbl from cable needle

2/2 RKT: Slip next 2 sts to cable needle and place at back of work, k2tbl, then k2 from cable needle

2/2 LPT: Slip next 2 sts to cable needle and place at front of work, p2, then k2tbl from cable needle

2/2 RPT: Slip next 2 sts to cable needle and place at back of work, k2tbl, then p2 from cable needle

See full list of abbreviations on page 84.

SOCK ONE

CUFF AND LEG

Cast on 62 (72, 82) sts. Join to work in the round, being careful not to twist. Place marker for start of round.

Set-up round: *P2, k2, p2, k2tbl, p2, k1tbl, p1, k1tbl, p2, k2tbl, p2, k2, [p2, k1tbl, p1, k1tbl] 2 (3, 4) times; rep from * once more.

Round 1: *P2, reading from right to left, work 19 sts from row 1 of chart A, [p2, k1tbl, k1, k1tbl] 2 (3, 4) times; rep from * once more.
Round 2: *P2, reading from right to left, work 19 sts from row 2 of chart A, [p2, k1tbl, p1, k1tbl] 2 (3, 4) times; rep from * once more.
Last 2 rounds set broken twisted rib and chart A patterns. Working next row of chart A each time, continue as set until chart A has been completed once and rounds 1-16 have been worked once more (36 rounds).

Round 37: P2, reading from right to left, work 19 sts from row 1 of chart B, [p2,

k1tbl, k1, k1tbl] 2 (3, 4) times, p2, reading from right to left, work 19 sts from row 17 of chart A, [p2, k1tbl, k1, k1tbl] 2 (3, 4) times.

Round 38: P2, reading from right to left, work 19 sts from row 2 of chart B, [p2, k1tbl, p1, k1tbl] 2 (3, 4) times, reading from right to left, work 19 sts from row 18 of chart A, [p2, k1tbl, p1, k1tbl] 2 (3, 4) times. Last 2 rounds set broken twisted rib and charts A and B. Working next row of charts each time, continue as set until row 34 of chart B has been completed (ending with row 10 of chart A) (34 rounds).

HEEL FLAP

Turn work so WS is facing. Heel flap will be worked back and forth on the next 29 (34, 39) sts beginning with a WS row. Keep remaining 33 (38, 43) sts on needles for instep.

Row 1 (WS): Sl1 wyif, p28 (33, 38).
Row 2 (RS): *Sl1 wyib, k1; rep from * to last 1 (0, 1) st, k1 (0, 1).
Rep the last 2 rows a further 14 times then work row 1 once more.

Pattern continues on page 61.

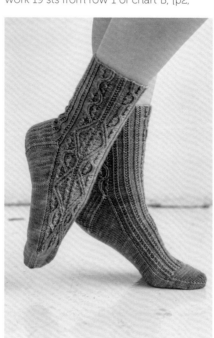

Charts

CHART B

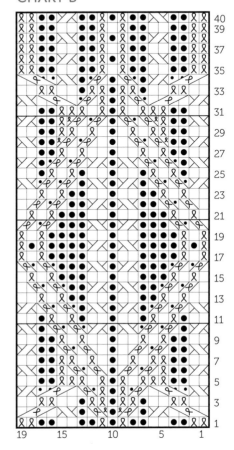

CHART A

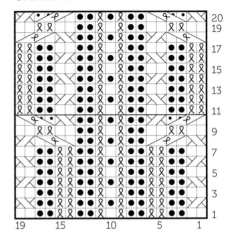

KEY

☐ knit

● purl

⚇ k1tbl

1/1 LC: Slip next st to cable needle and place at front of work, k1, then k1 from cable needle.

1/1 RC: Slip next st to cable needle and place at back of work, k1, then k1 from cable needle.

1/1 LT: Slip next st to cable needle and place at front of work, k1tbl, then k1tbl from cable needle.

1/1 RT: Slip next st to cable needle and place at back of work, k1tbl, then k1tbl from cable needle.

1/1 LKT: Slip next st to cable needle and place at front of work, k1, then k1tbl from cable needle.

1/1 RKT: Slip next st to cable needle and place at back of work, k1tbl, then k1 from cable needle.

1/1 LPT: Slip next st to cable needle and place at front of work, p1, then k1tbl from cable needle.

1/1 RPT: Slip next st to cable needle and place at back of work, k1tbl, then p1 from cable needle.

2/2 LKT: Slip next 2 sts to cable needle and place at front of work, k2, then k2tbl from cable needle.

2/2 RKT: Slip next 2 sts to cable needle and place at back of work, k2tbl, then k2 from cable needle.

2/2 LPT: Slip next 2 sts to cable needle and place at front of work, p2, then k2tbl from cable needle.

2/2 RPT: Slip next 2 sts to cable needle and place at back of work, k2tbl, then p2 from cable needle.

Pattern continues:

HEEL TURN

Row 1 (RS): Sl1 wyib, k15 (18, 21), ssk, k1, turn, leaving remaining 10 (12, 14) sts unworked.

Row 2 (WS): Sl1 wyif, p4 (5, 6), p2tog, p1, turn, leaving remaining 10 (12, 14) sts unworked.

Row 3: Sl1 wyib, knit to 1 st before gap, ssk, k1, turn.

Row 4: Sl1 wyif, purl to 1 st before gap, p2tog, p1, turn.

Rep last 2 rows a further 4 (5, 6) times. All heel sts have been worked. 17 (20, 23) heel sts remain.

GUSSET

Begin working in the round again as follows:

Set-up round: Sl1 wyib, k16 (19, 22), pick up and knit 16 sts along edge of heel flap (1 st in each slipped st along edge of flap), work across 33 (38, 43) instep sts as follows: P2, work 19 sts from row 35 of chart B, p2, [k1tbl, k1, k1tbl, p2] 2 (3, 4) times, pick up and knit 16 sts along edge of heel flap, k33 (36, 39). Place marker for new start of round (at start of instep sts). 82 (90, 98) sts.

Round 1: P2, work 19 sts from row 36 of chart B, p2, [k1tbl, p1, k1tbl, p2] 2 (3, 4) times, ssk, knit to last 2 sts, k2tog. 2 sts dec.

Round 2: P2, work 19 sts from row 37 of chart B, p2, [k1tbl, k1, k1tbl, p2] 2 (3, 4) times, knit to end.

Working next row of chart each time, rep last 2 rounds a further 8 (7, 6) times. 18 (16, 14) sts dec; 64 (74, 84) sts.

You now have 33 (38, 43) sts on instep and 31 (36, 41) sts on sole.

FOOT

Work as set (broken twisted rib and chart B on instep and st st on sole) until the sock measures 5 (5.5, 6.5) cm [2 (2¼, 2½) in] less than the desired foot length.

Toe set-up round: K1, ssk, k27 (32, 37), k2tog, knit to end. 62 (72, 82) sts remain.

Eula

TOE
Round 1: Knit.
Round 2: K1, ssk, k25 (30, 35), k2tog, k1, pm, k1, ssk, knit to last 3 sts, k2tog, k1. 58 (68, 78) sts.
Round 3: Knit.
Round 4: *K1, ssk, knit to 3 sts before marker, k2tog, k1, slm; rep from * once more. 4 sts dec.
Rep last 2 rounds a further 9 (10, 12) times. 40 (44, 52) sts dec; 18 (24, 26) sts remain.
Cut yarn, leaving a 30cm [12in] tail. Graft sts together using Kitchener stitch. Weave in ends.

SOCK TWO

LEG
Cast on 62 (72, 82) sts. Join to work in the round, being careful not to twist. Place marker for start of round.

Set-up round: *[P2, k1tbl, p1, k1tbl] 2 (3, 4) times, p2, k2, p2, k2tbl, p2, k1tbl, p1, k1tbl, p2, k2tbl, p2, k2; rep from * once more.

Round 1: *[P2, k1tbl, k1, k1tbl] 2 (3, 4) times, p2, reading from right to left, work 19 sts from row 1 of chart A; rep from * once more.
Round 2: *[P2, k1tbl, p1, k1tbl] 2 (3, 4) times, p2, reading from right to left, work 19 sts from row 2 of chart A; rep from * once more.
Last 2 rounds set broken twisted rib and chart A patterns. Working next row of chart A each time, continue as set until

chart A has been completed once and rounds 1-16 have been worked once more (36 rounds).

Round 37: [P2, k1tbl, k1, k1tbl] 2 (3, 4) times, p2, reading from right to left, work 19 sts from row 1 of chart B, [p2, k1tbl, k1, k1tbl] 2 (3, 4) times, p2, reading from right to left, work 19 sts from row 17 of chart A.
Round 38: [P2, k1tbl, p1, k1tbl] 2 (3, 4) times, p2, reading from right to left, work 19 sts from row 2 of chart B, [p2, k1tbl, p1, k1tbl] 2 (3, 4) times, p2, reading from right to left, work 19 sts from row 18 of chart A.
Last 2 rounds set broken twisted rib and charts A and B. Working next row of charts each time, continue as set until row 34 of chart B has been completed (ending with row 10 of chart A) (34 rounds).

HEEL FLAP AND TURN
Work as Sock One.

GUSSET
Begin working in the round again as follows:
Set-up round: Sl1 wyib, k16 (19, 22), pick up and knit 16 sts along edge of heel flap (1 st in each slipped st along edge of flap), work across 33 (38, 43) instep sts as follows: P2, [k1tbl, k1, k1tbl, p2] 2 (3, 4) times, work 19 sts from row 35 of chart B, p2, pick up and knit 16 sts along edge of heel flap, k33 (36, 39). Place marker for new start of round (at start of instep sts). 82 (90, 98) sts.

Round 1: P2, [k1tbl, p1, k1tbl, p2] 2 (3, 4) times, work 19 sts from row 36 of chart B, p2, ssk, knit to last 2 sts, k2tog. 2 sts dec.
Round 2: P2, [k1tbl, k1, k1tbl, p2] 2 (3, 4) times, work 19 sts from row 37 of chart B, p2, knit to end.
Working next row of chart each time, rep last 2 rounds a further 8 (7, 6) times. 18 (16, 14) sts dec; 64 (74, 84) sts.

You now have 33 (38, 43) sts on instep and 31 (36, 41) sts on sole.

FOOT AND TOE
Work as Sock One.

WRITTEN CHART INSTRUCTIONS

CHART A

19 STS AND 20 ROUNDS

Round 1: K2, p2, k2tbl, p2, k1tbl, k1, k1tbl, p2, k2tbl, p2, k2.

Round 2: 1/1 RC, p2, k2tbl, p2, k1tbl, p1, k1tbl, p2, k2tbl, p2, 1/1 LC.

Round 3: Rep round 1.

Round 4: 1/1 LC, p2, k2tbl, p2, k1tbl, p1, k1tbl, p2, k2tbl, p2, 1/1 RC.

Round 5: Rep round 1.

Round 6: Rep round 2.

Round 7: Rep round 1.

Round 8: 1/1 LC, 2/2 RKT, p2, k1tbl, p1, k1tbl, p2, 2/2 LKT, 1/1 RC.

Round 9: K2, k2tbl, k2, p2, k1tbl, k1, k1tbl, p2, k2, k2tbl, k2.

Round 10: 2/2 RPT, 1/1 RC, p2, k1tbl, p1, k1tbl, p2, 1/1 LC, 2/2 LPT.

Round 11: K2tbl, p2, k2, p2, k1tbl, k1, k1tbl, p2, k2, p2, k2tbl.

Round 12: K2tbl, p2, 1/1 LC, p2, k1tbl, p1, k1tbl, p2, 1/1 RC, p2, k2tbl.

Round 13: Rep round 11.

Round 14: K2tbl, p2, 1/1 RC, p2, k1tbl, p1, k1tbl, p2, 1/1 LC, p2, k2tbl.

Round 15: Rep round 11.

Round 16: Rep round 12.

Round 17: Rep round 11.

Round 18: 2/2 LKT, 1/1 RC, p2, k1tbl, p1, k1tbl, p2, 1/1 LC, 2/2 RKT.

Round 19: Rep round 9.

Round 20: 1/1 LC, 2/2 LPT, p2, k1tbl, p1, k1tbl, p2, 2/2 RPT, 1/1 RC.

CHART B

19 STS AND 40 ROUNDS

Round 1: K2tbl, p2, k2, p2, k1tbl, p1, k1tbl, p2, k2, p2, k2tbl.

Round 2: 2/2 LKT, 1/1 RC, p1, 1/1 RT, p1, 1/1 LT, p1, 1/1 LC, 2/2 RKT.

Round 3: K2, k2tbl, k2, [p1, k2tbl] twice, p1, k2, k2tbl, k2.

Round 4: 1/1 LC, 2/2 LPT, 1/1 RPT, k1tbl, p1, k1tbl, 1/1 LPT, 2/2 RPT, 1/1 RC.

Round 5: K2, p2, k3tbl, k1, k1tbl, p1, k1tbl, k1, k3tbl, p2, k2.

Round 6: 1/1 RC, p2, k1tbl, 1/1 RPT, 1/1 RKT, p1, 1/1 LKT, 1/1 LPT, k1tbl, p2, 1/1 LC.

Round 7: K2, p2, k2tbl, k1, k1tbl, k1, p1, k1, k1tbl, k1, k2tbl, p2, k2.

Round 8: 1/1 LC, p2, 1/1 RPT, 1/1 RKT, k1, p1, k1, 1/1 LKT, 1/1 LPT, p2, 1/1 RC.

Round 9: K2, p2, k1tbl, k1, k1tbl, k2, p1, k2, k1tbl, k1, k1tbl, p2, k2.

Round 10: 1/1 RC, p1, [1/1 RPT] twice, 1/1 LC, p1, 1/1 RC, [1/1 LPT] twice, p1, 1/1 LC.

Round 11: K2, p1, k1tbl, k1, k1tbl, [p1, k2] twice, p1, k1tbl, k1, k1tbl, p1, k2.

Round 12: 1/1 LC, [1/1 RPT] twice, p1, 1/1 RC, p1, 1/1 LC, p1, [1/1 LPT] twice, 1/1 RC.

Round 13: K2, k2tbl, k1, k1tbl, p2, k2, p1, k2, p2, k1tbl, k1, k1tbl, k2.

Round 14: K1, [1/1 RPT] twice, p2, 1/1 LC, p1, 1/1 RC, p2, [1/1 LPT] twice, k1.

Round 15: [K1, k1tbl] twice, p3, k2, p1, k2, p3, [k1tbl, k1] twice.

Round 16: [1/1 RPT] twice, p3, 1/1 RC, p1, 1/1 LC, p3, [1/1 LPT] twice.

Round 17: K1tbl, k1, k1tbl, p4, k2, p1, k2, p4, k1tbl, k1, k1tbl.

Round 18: K1tbl, p1, k1tbl, p4, 1/1 LC, p1, 1/1 RC, p4, k1tbl, p1, k1tbl.

Round 19: Rep round 17.

Round 20: 1/1 LKT, 1/1 LPT, p3, 1/1 RC, p1, 1/1 LC, p3, 1/1 RPT, 1/1 RKT.

Round 21: Rep round 15.

Round 22: K1, 1/1 LKT, 1/1 LPT, p2, 1/1 LC, p1, 1/1 RC, p2, 1/1 RPT, 1/1 RKT, k1.

Round 23: Rep round 13.

Round 24: 1/1 RC, [1/1 LPT] twice, p1, 1/1 RC, p1, 1/1 LC, p1, [1/1 RPT] twice, 1/1 LC.

Round 25: Rep round 11.

Round 26: 1/1 LC, p1, [1/1 LPT] twice, 1/1 LC, p1, 1/1 RC, [1/1 RPT] twice, p1, 1/1 RC.

Round 27: Rep round 9.

Round 28: 1/1 RC, p2, 1/1 LT, 1/1 LPT, k1, p1, k1, 1/1 RPT, 1/1 RT, p2, 1/1 LC.

Round 29: Rep round 7.

Round 30: 1/1 LC, p2, k1tbl, 1/1 LT, 1/1 LPT, p1, 1/1 RPT, 1/1 RT, k1tbl, p2, 1/1 RC.

Round 31: Rep round 5.

Round 32: 1/1 RC, 2/2 RKT, 1/1 LPT, k1tbl, p1, k1tbl, 1/1 RPT, 2/2 LKT, 1/1 LC.

Round 33: Rep round 3.

Round 34: 2/2 RPT, 1/1 RC, p1, 1/1 LPT, p1, 1/1 RPT, p1, 1/1 LC, 2/2 LPT.

Round 35: K2tbl, p2, k2, p2, k1tbl, k1, k1tbl, p2, k2, p2, k2tbl.

Round 36: K2tbl, p2, 1/1 LC, p2, k1tbl, p1, k1tbl, p2, 1/1 RC, p2, k2tbl.

Round 37: Rep round 35.

Round 38: K2tbl, p2, 1/1 RC, p2, k1tbl, p1, k1tbl, p2, 1/1 LC, p2, k2tbl.

Round 39: Rep round 35.

Round 40: Rep round 36.

his rib pattern works well for both men and women, and features an extended version of the openwork design on the foot.

Ernestine
sock of my heart !

Ernestine

YARN
Blue Version: Babylonglegs Flump Merino Sock (100% superwash merino; 366m [400yds] per 100g skein) 1 skein in Silver Surfer
Brown Version: Fyberspates Vivacious 4ply (100% superwash merino; 365m [399yds] per 100g skein) 1 skein in Silver and Bronze

NEEDLES
2.5mm [UK 13-12/US 1-2] 80cm [32in] circular needles or DPNs (or size needed to get correct tension)
Stitch markers
Tapestry needle

TENSION
36 sts and 50 rounds = 10cm [4in] over st st
38 sts and 50 rounds = 10cm [4in] over lace rib pattern (unstretched)

SIZES
Small (Medium, Large)
To fit foot circumference: 20.5 (23, 25.5) cm [8 (9, 10) in]
Actual foot circumference of sock (unstretched): 18 (20, 22) cm [7 (7¾, 8¾) in]
Length of leg to top of heel flap: 15cm [6in]
Foot length is fully adjustable within the pattern.
Finished sock measures 0.5cm [¼in] less than actual foot length, to ensure a good fit.

PATTERN NOTES
The charted stitch patterns are also given as written instructions at the end of the pattern.

ABBREVIATIONS
See full list of abbreviations on page 84.

SOCK ONE

CUFF

Cast on 64 (72, 80) sts. Join to work in the round, being careful not to twist. Place marker for start of round.

Round 1: *K1, p2, k1; rep from * to end. Work this round a further 15 times (16 rounds).

LEG

Round 1: Reading from right to left, [work 8 sts from row 1 of chart A] 8 (9, 10) times. Last round sets lace rib pattern. Working next row of chart A each time, continue in pattern as set until chart A has been completed 3 times and rounds 1-11 have been worked once more (59 rounds).

HEEL FLAP

Turn work so WS is facing. Heel flap will be worked back and forth on the next 32 (36, 40) sts beginning with a WS row. Keep remaining 32 (36, 40) sts on needles for instep.

Row 1 (WS): Sl1 wyif, p31 (35, 39).
Row 2 (RS): *Sl1 wyib, k1; rep from * to end. Rep the last 2 rows a further 14 times then work row 1 once more.

HEEL TURN

Row 1 (RS): Sl1 wyib, k18 (20, 22), ssk, k1, turn, leaving remaining 10 (12, 14) sts unworked.
Row 2 (WS): Sl1 wyif, p7, p2tog, p1, turn, leaving remaining 10 (12, 14) sts unworked.
Row 3: Sl1 wyib, knit to 1 st before gap, ssk, k1, turn.
Row 4: Sl1 wyif, purl to 1 st before gap, p2tog, p1, turn.
Rep last 2 rows a further 4 (5, 6) times. All heel sts have been worked. 20 (22, 24) heel sts remain.

GUSSET

Begin working in the round again as follows:
Set-up round: Sl1 wyib, k19 (21, 23), pick up and knit 16 sts along edge of heel flap (1 st in each slipped st along edge of flap), k32 (36, 40) instep sts (for row 1 of chart), pick up and knit 16 sts along edge of heel flap, k36 (38, 40). Place marker for new start of round (at start of instep sts). 84 (90, 96) sts.

SMALL AND LARGE SIZES

Round 1: [Work row 2 of chart B] 4 (-, 5) times, ssk, knit to last 2 sts, k2tog. 2 sts dec.
Round 2: [Work row 3 of chart B] 4 (-, 5) times, knit to end.

MEDIUM SIZE ONLY

Round 1: Work from row 2 of chart C, repeating marked section 4 times in total, ssk, knit to last 2 sts, k2tog. 2 sts dec.
Round 2: Work from row 3 of chart C, repeating marked section 4 times in total, knit to end.

ALL SIZES

Working next row of charts each time, rep last 2 rounds a further 9 (8, 7) times. 20 (18, 16) sts dec; 64 (72, 80) sts remain. You now have 32 (36, 40) sts each on instep and on sole.

FOOT

Work as set (charts on instep and st st on sole) until the sock measures 5.5 (6, 6.5) cm [2¼ (2¼, 2½) in] less than the desired foot length.

TOE

Round 1: Knit.
Round 2: K1, ssk, k26 (30, 34), k2tog, k1, pm, k1, ssk, knit to last 3 sts, k2tog, k1. 60 (68, 76) sts.
Round 3: Knit.
Round 4: *K1, ssk, knit to 3 sts before marker, k2tog, k1, slm; rep from * once more. 4 sts dec.

Ernestine

Charts

KEY

- ☐ knit
- ● purl
- ⍟ k1tbl
- ◳ ssk
- ◲ k2tog
- ◎ yarnover
- ☐ pattern repeat

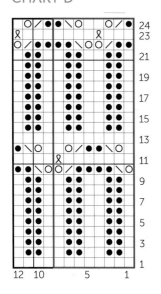

CHART D

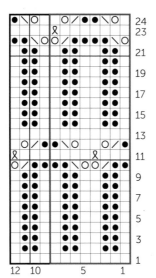

CHART C

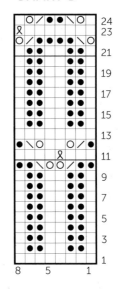

CHART B

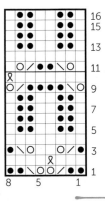

CHART A

Pattern continues:

Rep last 2 rounds a further 9 (10, 12) times. 40 (44, 52) sts dec; 20 (24, 24) sts remain. Cut yarn, leaving a 30cm [12in] tail. Graft sts together using Kitchener stitch. Weave in ends.

SOCK TWO
SMALL AND LARGE SIZES
Work entire sock as Sock One.

MEDIUM SIZE ONLY
Work as follows:

CUFF AND LEG
Work as Sock One.

HEEL SET-UP
MEDIUM SIZE ONLY
Heel set up (partial round): Remove marker, k4. This ensures the heel flap is correctly positioned.

HEEL FLAP AND TURN
Work as Sock One.

GUSSET
MEDIUM SIZE ONLY
Begin working in the round again as follows:

Set-up round: Sl1 wyib, k21, pick up and knit 16 sts along edge of heel flap (1 st in each slipped st along edge of flap), k36 instep sts, pick up and knit 16 sts along edge of heel flap, k38. Place marker for new start of round (at start of instep sts). 90 sts.

Round 1: Work from row 2 of chart D, repeating marked section 4 times in total, ssk, knit to last 2 sts, k2tog. 2 sts dec.
Round 2: Work from row 3 of chart D, repeating marked section 4 times in total, knit to end.
Working next row of chart D each time, rep last 2 rounds a further 8 times. 18 sts dec; 72 sts remain.
You now have 36 sts each on instep and on sole.

FOOT AND TOE
Work as Sock One.

WRITTEN CHART INSTRUCTIONS

CHART A
8 STS AND 16 ROUNDS
Round 1: P2, k2tog, [yo] twice, ssk, p2.
Round 2: K3, k1tbl, k4.
Round 3: P1, k2tog, yo, k2, yo, ssk, p1.
Round 4: Knit.
Rounds 5-8: K1, p2, k2, p2, k1.
Round 9: Yo, ssk, p4, k2tog, yo.
Round 10: K7, k1tbl.
Round 11: K1, yo, ssk, p2, k2tog, yo, k1.
Round 12: Knit.
Rounds 13-16: Rep rounds 5-8.

CHART B
8 STS AND 24 ROUNDS
Round 1: Knit.
Rounds 2-9: K1, p2, k2, p2, k1.
Round 10: P2, k2tog, [yo] twice, ssk, p2.
Round 11: K3, k1tbl, k4.
Round 12: P1, k2tog, yo, k2, yo, ssk, p1.
Round 13: Knit.
Rounds 14-21: Rep rounds 2-9.
Round 22: Yo, ssk, p4, k2tog, yo.
Round 23: K7, k1tbl.
Round 24: K1, yo, ssk, p2, k2tog, yo, k1.

CHART C
MULTIPLE OF 8 + 4 STS AND 24 ROUNDS
Repeat instructions from * to * as indicated in the pattern.
Round 1: Knit.
Rounds 2-9: *K1, p2, k2, p2, k1*, k1, p2, k1.
Round 10: *P2, k2tog, [yo] twice, ssk, p2*, p2, k2tog, yo.
Round 11: *K3, k1tbl, k4*, k3, k1tbl.
Round 12: *P1, k2tog, yo, k2, yo, ssk, p1*, p1, k2tog, yo, k1.
Round 13: Knit.
Rounds 14-21: Rep rounds 2-9.
Round 22: *Yo, ssk, p4, k2tog, yo*, yo, ssk, p2.
Round 23: *K7, k1tbl*, k4.
Round 24: *K1, yo, ssk, p2, k2tog, yo, k1*, k1, yo, ssk, p1.

CHART D
MULTIPLE OF 8 + 4 STS AND 24 ROUNDS
Repeat instructions from * to * as indicated in the pattern.
Round 1: Knit.
Rounds 2-9: *K1, p2, k2, p2, k1*, k1, p2, k1.
Round 10: *Yo, ssk, p4, k2tog, yo*, yo, ssk, p2.
Round 11: *K7, k1tbl*, k4.
Round 12: *K1, yo, ssk, p2, k2tog, yo, k1*, k1, yo, ssk, p1.
Round 13: Knit.
Rounds 14-21: Rep rounds 2-9.
Round 22: *P2, k2tog, [yo] twice, ssk, p2*, p2, k2tog, yo.
Round 23: *K3, k1tbl, k4*, k3, k1tbl.
Round 24: *P1, k2tog, yo, k2, yo, ssk, p1*, p1, k2tog, yo, k1.

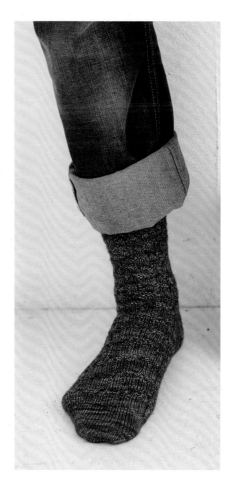

Wilbert

king of socks

Braided cable ropes combine with a neat lace pattern, lending Wilbert a smart, nautical air.

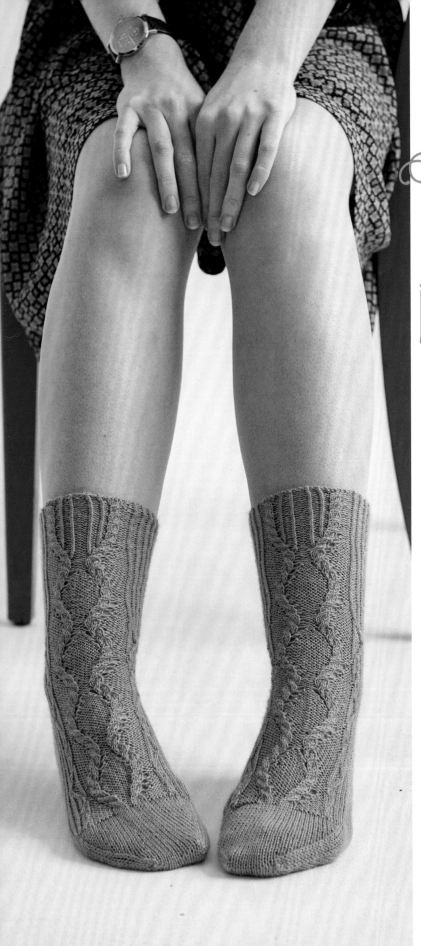

Wilbert

YARN
Yellow Version: Eden Cottage Yarns Milburn 4ply (85% wool, 15% silk; 199m [218yds] per 50g skein) 2 skeins in Mustard
Green Version: Old Maiden Aunt Yarns Superwash Merino 4ply (100% superwash merino; 366m [400yds] per 100g skein) 1 skein in Bean Nighe

NEEDLES
2.5mm [UK 13-12/US 1-2] 80cm [32in] circular needles or DPNs (or size needed to get correct tension)
Cable needle
Stitch markers
Tapestry needle

TENSION
36 sts and 50 rounds = 10cm [4in] over st st
46 sts and 50 rounds = 10cm [4in] over twisted rib (unstretched)
22 sts = 4.5cm [1¾in] over chart C cable pattern

SIZES
Small (Medium, Large)
To fit foot circumference: 20.5 (23, 25.5) cm [8 (9, 10) in]
Actual foot circumference of sock (unstretched): 14 (16, 18) cm [5½ (6¼, 7) in]
Length of leg to top of heel flap: 15cm [6in]
Foot length is fully adjustable within the pattern.
Finished sock measures 0.5cm [¼in] less than actual foot length, to ensure a good fit.

PATTERN NOTES
The charted stitch patterns are also given as written instructions at the end of the pattern.

ABBREVIATIONS

1/1 LT: Slip next st to cable needle and place at front of work, k1tbl, then k1tbl from cable needle

1/1 RT: Slip next st to cable needle and place at back of work, k1tbl, then k1tbl from cable needle

1/1 LPT: Slip next st to cable needle and place at front of work, p1, then k1tbl from cable needle

1/1 RPT: Slip next st to cable needle and place at back of work, k1tbl, then p1 from cable needle

2/2 LC: Slip next 2 sts to cable needle and place at front of work, k2, then k2 from cable needle

2/2 RC: Slip next 2 sts to cable needle and place at back of work, k2, then k2 from cable needle

See full list of abbreviations on page 84.

CUFF

Cast on 66 (74, 82) sts. Join to work in the round, being careful not to twist. Place marker for start of round.

Round 1: [P1, k1tbl] 3 (4, 5) times, reading from right to left, work 22 sts from row 1 of chart A, [k1tbl, p1] 5 (7, 9) times, k1tbl, reading from right to left, work 22 sts from row 1 of chart A, [k1tbl, p1] 2 (3, 4) times, k1tbl.
Last round sets rib and chart patterns. Working next row of chart each time, continue in pattern as set until chart A has been completed 5 times (20 rounds).

LEG

Round 1: [P1, k1tbl] 3 (4, 5) times, reading from right to left, work 22 sts from row 1 of chart B, [k1tbl, p1] 5 (7, 9) times, k1tbl, reading from right to left, work 22 sts from row 1 of chart B, [k1tbl, p1] 2 (3, 4) times, k1tbl.
Last round sets rib and chart patterns. Working next row of charts each time, continue in pattern as set until chart B has been completed once (7 rounds).

Round 8: [P1, k1tbl] 3 (4, 5) times, work 22 sts from row 1 of chart C, [k1tbl, p1] 5 (7, 9) times, k1tbl, work 22 sts from row 1 of chart C, [k1tbl, p1] 2 (3, 4) times, k1tbl.
Last round sets rib and chart patterns. Working next row of chart each time, continue in pattern as set until chart C has been completed once (24 rounds).

SMALL SIZE ONLY

Round 32: *P1, work 32 sts from row 1 of chart D; rep from * once more.

MEDIUM SIZE ONLY

Round 32: *P1, k1tbl, p1, work 32 sts from row 1 of chart D, p1, k1tbl; rep from * once more.

LARGE SIZE ONLY

Round 32: *P1, [k1tbl, p1] twice, work 32 sts from row 1 of chart D, [p1, k1tbl] twice; rep from * once more.

ALL SIZES

Last round sets rib and chart patterns. Working next row of charts each time, continue in pattern as set until chart D has been completed once (24 rounds).

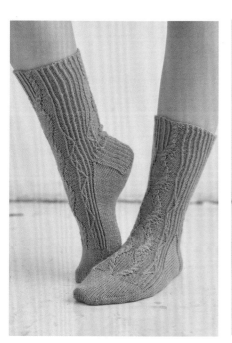
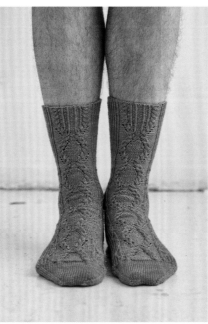

Wilbert

Charts

CHART D

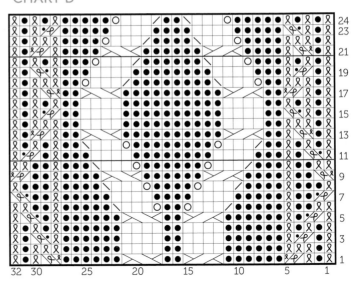

CHART C

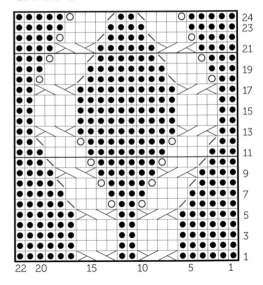

CHART B

CHART A

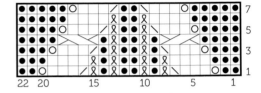

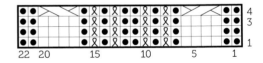

KEY

☐ knit

● purl

⊠ k1tbl

╲ ssk

╱ k2tog

○ yarnover

1/1 LT: Slip next st to cable needle and place at front of work, k1tbl, then k1tbl from cable needle.

1/1 RT: Slip next st to cable needle and place at back of work, k1tbl, then k1tbl from cable needle.

1/1 LPT: Slip next st to cable needle and place at front of work, p1, then k1tbl from cable needle.

1/1 RPT: Slip next st to cable needle and place at back of work, k1tbl, then p1 from cable needle.

2/2 LC: Slip next 2 sts to cable needle and place at front of work, k2, then k2 from cable needle.

2/2 RC: Slip next 2 sts to cable needle and place at back of work, k2, then k2 from cable needle.

Wilbert

Pattern continues:

HEEL FLAP

Turn work so WS is facing. Heel flap will be worked back and forth on the next 32 (36, 40) sts beginning with a WS row. Keep remaining 34 (38, 42) sts on needles for instep.

Row 1 (WS): Sl1 wyif, p31 (35, 39).
Row 2 (RS): *Sl1 wyib, k1; rep from * to end.
Rep the last 2 rows a further 14 times then work row 1 once more.

HEEL TURN

Row 1 (RS): Sl1 wyib, k18 (20, 22), ssk, k1, turn, leaving remaining 10 (12, 14) sts unworked.
Row 2 (WS): Sl1 wyif, p7, p2tog, p1, turn, leaving remaining 10 (12, 14) sts unworked.
Row 3: Sl1 wyib, knit to 1 st before gap, ssk, k1, turn.
Row 4: Sl1 wyif, purl to 1 st before gap, p2tog, p1, turn.
Rep last 2 rows a further 4 (5, 6) times. All heel sts have been worked. 20 (22, 24) heel sts remain.

GUSSET

Begin working in the round again as follows:

Set-up round: Sl1 wyib, k19 (21, 23), pick up and knit 16 sts along edge of heel flap (1 st in each slipped st along edge of flap), work across 34 (38, 42) instep sts as follows and as previously est: P1, [k1tbl, p1] 0 (1, 2) times, work 32 sts from row 1 of chart D, p1, [k1tbl, p1] 0 (1, 2) times, pick up and knit 16 sts along edge of heel flap, k36 (38, 40). Place marker for new start of round (at start of instep sts). 86 (92, 98) sts.

Round 1: P1, [k1tbl, p1] 0 (1, 2) times, work 32 sts from row 2 of chart D, p1, [k1tbl, p1] 0 (1, 2) times, ssk, knit to last 2 sts, k2tog. 2 sts dec.
Round 2: P1, [k1tbl, p1] 0 (1, 2) times, work 32 sts from row 3 of chart D, p1, [k1tbl, p1] 0 (1, 2) times, knit to end.
Working next row of chart each time, rep last 2 rounds a further 9 (8, 7) times. 20 (18, 16) sts dec; 66 (74, 82) sts remain.

You now have 34 (38, 42) sts on instep and 32 (36, 40) sts on sole.

FOOT

Work as set (twisted rib and chart D on instep and st st on sole) until the sock measures 5 (5.5, 6.5) cm [2 (2¼, 2½) in] less than the desired foot length.

Toe set-up round: K1, ssk, k28 (32, 36), k2tog, knit to end. 2 sts dec; 64 (72, 80) sts remain.

TOE

Round 1: Knit.
Round 2: K1, ssk, k26 (30, 34), k2tog, k1, pm, k1, ssk, knit to last 3 sts, k2tog, k1. 60 (68, 76) sts.
Round 3: Knit.
Round 4: *K1, ssk, knit to 3 sts before marker, k2tog, k1, slm; rep from * once more. 4 sts dec.
Rep last 2 rounds a further 9 (10, 12) times. 40 (44, 52) sts dec; 20 (24, 24) sts remain.
Cut yarn, leaving a 30cm [12in] tail. Graft sts together using Kitchener stitch. Weave in ends.

Written chart instructions appear on the following page.

Wilbert

WRITTEN CHART INSTRUCTIONS

CHART A
22 STS AND 4 ROUNDS

Rounds 1-3: P2, k4, [p1, k1tbl] twice, p2, [k1tbl, p1] twice, k4, p2.
Round 4: P2, 2/2 RC, [p1, k1tbl] twice, p2, [k1tbl, p1] twice, 2/2 LC, p2.

CHART B
22 STS AND 7 ROUNDS

Round 1: P2, yo, k3, ssk, k1tbl, p1, k1tbl, p2, k1tbl, p1, k1tbl, k2tog, k3, yo, p2.
Round 2: P3, k4, k1tbl, p1, k1tbl, p2, k1tbl, p1, k1tbl, k4, p3.
Round 3: P3, yo, k3, ssk, p1, k1tbl, p2, k1tbl, p1, k2tog, k3, yo, p3.
Round 4: P4, 2/2 RC, p1, k1tbl, p2, k1tbl, p1, 2/2 LC, p4.
Round 5: P4, yo, k3, ssk, k1tbl, p2, k1tbl, k2tog, k3, yo, p4.
Round 6: P5, k4, k1tbl, p2, k1tbl, k4, p5.
Round 7: P5, yo, k3, ssk, p2, k2tog, k3, yo, p5.

CHART C
22 STS AND 24 ROUNDS

Round 1: P6, 2/2 RC, p2, 2/2 LC, p6.
Rounds 2-4: P6, k4, p2, k4, p6.
Round 5: Rep round 1.
Round 6: P5, k2tog, k3, yo, p2, yo, k3, ssk, p5.
Round 7: P5, k4, p4, k4, p5.
Round 8: P4, k2tog, k3, yo, p4, yo, k3, ssk, p4.
Round 9: P4, 2/2 RC, p6, 2/2 LC, p4.
Round 10: P3, k2tog, k3, yo, p6, yo, k3, ssk, p3.
Round 11: P3, k4, p8, k4, p3.
Round 12: P2, k2tog, k3, yo, p8, yo, k3, ssk, p2.
Round 13: P2, 2/2 RC, p10, 2/2 LC, p2.
Rounds 14-16: P2, k4, p10, k4, p2.
Round 17: Rep round 13.
Round 18: P2, yo, k3, ssk, p8, k2tog, k3, yo, p2.
Round 19: Rep round 11.
Round 20: P3, yo, k3, ssk, p6, k2tog, k3, yo, p3.
Round 21: Rep round 9.
Round 22: P4, yo, k3, ssk, p4, k2tog, k3, yo, p4.
Round 23: Rep round 7.
Round 24: P5, yo, k3, ssk, p2, k2tog, k3, yo, p5.

CHART D
32 STS AND 24 ROUNDS

Round 1: K1tbl, p1, k1tbl, 1/1 RT, p6, 2/2 RC, p2, 2/2 LC, p6, 1/1 LT, k1tbl, p1, k1tbl.
Round 2: K1tbl, p1, k3tbl, p6, k4, p2, k4, p6, k3tbl, p1, k1tbl.
Round 3: K1tbl, p1, 1/1 RPT, k1tbl, p6, k4, p2, k4, p6, k1tbl, 1/1 LPT, p1, k1tbl.
Round 4: [K1tbl, p1] twice, k1tbl, p6, k4, p2, k4, p6, [k1tbl, p1] twice, k1tbl.
Round 5: K1tbl, 1/1 RPT, p1, k1tbl, p6, 2/2 RC, p2, 2/2 LC, p6, k1tbl, p1, 1/1 LPT, k1tbl.
Round 6: K2tbl, p2, k1tbl, p5, k2tog, k3, yo, p2, yo, k3, ssk, p5, k1tbl, p2, k2tbl.
Round 7: 1/1 RPT, p2, k1tbl, p5, k4, p4, k4, p5, k1tbl, p2, 1/1 LPT.
Round 8: K1tbl, p3, k1tbl, p4, k2tog, k3, yo, p4, yo, k3, ssk, p4, k1tbl, p3, k1tbl.
Round 9: 1/1 LT, p2, k1tbl, p4, 2/2 RC, p6, 2/2 LC, p4, k1tbl, p2, 1/1 RT.
Round 10: K2tbl, p2, k1tbl, p3, k2tog, k3, yo, p6, yo, k3, ssk, p3, k1tbl, p2, k2tbl.
Round 11: K1tbl, 1/1 LPT, p1, k1tbl, p3, k4, p8, k4, p3, k1tbl, p1, 1/1 RPT, k1tbl.
Round 12: [K1tbl, p1] twice, k1tbl, p2, k2tog, k3, yo, p8, yo, k3, ssk, p2, [k1tbl, p1] twice, k1tbl.
Round 13: K1tbl, p1, 1/1 LT, k1tbl, p2, 2/2 RC, p10, 2/2 LC, p2, k1tbl, 1/1 RT, p1, k1tbl.
Round 14: K1tbl, p1, k3tbl, p2, k4, p10, k4, p2, k3tbl, p1, k1tbl.
Round 15: K1tbl, p1, k1tbl, 1/1 LPT, p2, k4, p10, k4, p2, 1/1 RPT, k1tbl, p1, k1tbl.
Round 16: [K1tbl, p1] twice, k1tbl, p2, k4, p10, k4, p2, [k1tbl, p1] twice, k1tbl.
Round 17: K1tbl, p1, k1tbl, 1/1 RT, p2, 2/2 RC, p10, 2/2 LC, p2, 1/1 LT, k1tbl, p1, k1tbl.
Round 18: K1tbl, p1, k3tbl, p2, yo, k3, ssk, p8, k2tog, k3, yo, p2, k3tbl, p1, k1tbl.
Round 19: K1tbl, p1, 1/1 RPT, k1tbl, p3, k4, p8, k4, p3, k1tbl, 1/1 LPT, p1, k1tbl.
Round 20: [K1tbl, p1] twice, k1tbl, p3, yo, k3, ssk, p6, k2tog, k3, yo, p3, [k1tbl, p1] twice, k1tbl.
Round 21: K1tbl, p1, 1/1 LT, k1tbl, p4, 2/2 RC, p6, 2/2 LC, p4, k1tbl, 1/1 RT, p1, k1tbl.
Round 22: K1tbl, p1, k3tbl, p4, yo, k3, ssk, p4, k2tog, k3, yo, p4, k3tbl, p1, k1tbl.
Round 23: K1tbl, p1, k1tbl, 1/1 LPT, p5, k4, p4, k4, p5, 1/1 RPT, k1tbl, p1, k1tbl.
Round 24: [K1tbl, p1] twice, k1tbl, p5, yo, k3, ssk, p2, k2tog, k3, yo, p5, [k1tbl, p1] twice, k1tbl.

Why knit socks?

You will often be asked why you would bother to knit socks when you could just buy a pair very easily for not very much money.

Here's my take...

» Socks are small and portable, making them perfect commuting or travel companions.
» Many knitters will have a sock project on the go as well as a larger garment, so that they have something to take along on trips outside the house.
» Hand-knitted socks are warmer and more comfortable than most shop-bought socks.
» Socks are also a good way to learn new techniques – they are small and reach the 'finished object' stage much more quickly than a garment.
» They are possibly the ideal use for the beautifully unique hand-dyed yarns that are available around the world.
» Most socks can be knitted from 100g of yarn or less.

I'm sure there are many (many) more reasons to knit socks – of course, the perfect answer to this question is always...

'Because I can!'

The following pages have some good tips to get the best results from your sock knitting adventures.

TOP TIPS FOR SOCK KNITTERS

Here are some of my top tips for knitting socks:

WORK AT A TIGHT TENSION

Make sure that your knitted fabric is firm. Working at a tight tension ensures that your socks will last longer and won't sag. When stitches in fabric are too large, the yarn moves around more and rubs against itself, which causes wear. I usually work at a stocking stitch tension of 36 sts and 50 rows to 10cm [4in], which gives a firm, hard-wearing fabric in most standard sock yarns.

CHOOSING YARNS: COLOURS

Most of my textured sock designs will require a solid or semi-solid coloured yarn. Too much variegation in the colours makes the texture patterns hard to see. When choosing yarns for colourwork socks, such as Otis, be sure to check that all shades are colourfast before casting on. You can do this by soaking a portion of your skein in tepid water and then pressing the damp yarn on some kitchen roll. If any colour comes off on the towel it may require further rinsing before you knit with it. If colour continues to bleed, contact the yarn company or dyer for further advice.

CHOOSING YARNS: FIBRES

Some sock yarns have a nylon content, this can help strengthen the socks and make them last longer. A sock yarn which is 100% wool and has no nylon can also wear well, so long as it is knitted at a firm tension. Sock yarns with a small amount of silk can also be very strong. Yarns that are specifically intended for socks are often spun tightly and made from blends that are well-suited to knitting socks.

CASTING ON

I recommend using the Long-Tail Cast-On Method when casting on for socks. This gives a firm, but stretchy edge to your cuff. You will find a step-by-step tutorial on page 82. There is also a link to an online video tutorial shown on the next page.

TENSION

Obtaining the correct tension (US: gauge) for both the stocking stitch and stitch patterns in your sock is vital to creating a sock that fits. The needle sizes given are suggestions. Every knitter is different, and the fact that your tension matches in stocking stitch does not guarantee that it will match in the pattern stitch. It may not seem worth knitting a separate swatch in the round, but please be sure to check that you are getting the correct tension once you have knitted 10cm [4in] of the main leg pattern. This will save you from having to rip out a whole sock later.

Once you have knitted 10cm [4in] of the main leg pattern, carefully measure the number of stitches and rows over the central 10cm [4in]. If you have the correct number of stitches and rows, you are using the correct sized needles. If you have too many stitches (and rows), you will need to start again with larger needles. If you have too few stitches (and rows), you will need to try smaller needles.

It is very important to match the tension given in *both* stitch patterns; the needle size that you use to do this does not matter. It is the tension that determines the finished size of your socks and how much yarn is used.

SOCK SIZING

The socks in this book are all designed with negative ease. This means that the socks have a smaller foot circumference than your feet do. All of the stitch patterns used are inherently stretchy, so to ensure that your socks don't sag, they need to be knitted a little smaller than your foot size.

You will notice that no foot lengths are given in the patterns. This is because all socks can be knitted to the exact foot length required. Very long foot lengths may require more yarn; all of the samples were knitted to a foot length of 23cm [9in]. If you don't know the foot length of your sock recipient, the sizing tables below may prove useful. Sizing varies considerably between manufacturers and countries, so the best method is to measure the foot.

WOMEN'S SHOE SIZES AND FOOT LENGTHS

UK	2	2.5	3	3.5	4	4.5	5	5.5	6	6.5	7	7.5	8	8.5
EU	35	35	35-36	36	36-37	37	37-38	38	38-39	39	39-40	40	40-41	41
US	4.5	5	5.5	6	6.5	7	7.5	8	8.5	9	9.5	10	10.5	10.5
cm	21.5	22	22.5	23	23	23.5	24	24	24.5	25	25.5	26	26.5	26.5
in	8½	8¾	8¾	9	9	9¼	9½	9½	9¾	9¾	10	10¼	10½	10½

MEN'S SHOE SIZES AND FOOT LENGTHS

UK	5.5	6	6.5	7	7.5	8	8.5	9	9.5	10	10.5	11	11.5	12
EU	38	38-39	39	39-40	40	40-41	41	42-43	43	43-44	44	44-45	45	46
US	8	8.5	9	9.5	10	10.5	10.5	10	10.5	11	11.5	12	12.5	13
cm	24	24.5	25	25.5	26	26.5	26.5	27	27	27.5	28	28.5	28.5	29
in	9½	9¾	9¾	10	10¼	10½	10½	10¾	10¾	10¾	11	11¼	11¼	11½

YARDAGE AND LARGER FEET

If you are knitting socks for a shoe size greater than a UK size 7 you will need to choose a sock yarn with a yardage of greater than 400m [438yds] or purchase two skeins, to ensure you will have enough yarn to complete your socks. The socks shown on female models in this book are a UK size 7 and the socks shown on a man are UK size 10.

WRITTEN INSTRUCTIONS

Where there is only one set of numbers in a pattern instruction, it refers to all sizes. When more than one number is given, the smallest size appears first, with the larger sizes appearing inside brackets in size order. It is always useful to circle or highlight the size you are working throughout the pattern before you start. Read the pattern carefully, as sometimes smaller groups of sizes are treated separately. It is always marked clearly where the instructions return to all sizes.

USING CHARTS

Charts are a graphical representation of your knitting, with each square representing a stitch (or small group of stitches) and every row of squares representing a round of knitting. All chart rows are read from right to left, since the sock designs in this book are all knitted in the round.

We have given written instructions for all of the non-colourwork charts in this book.

This article from Knitty.com is a helpful tutorial on knitting from charts: **www.tinyurl.com/KnittingCharts**

REPEATING INSTRUCTIONS

Where a pattern tells you to repeat from * a certain number more times, it means that you should work the instruction once, and then work it a further number of times as instructed. For example, *p1, k1 tbl; repeat from * a further 2 times. This means that you repeat "p1, k1 tbl" three times in total (p1, k1 tbl, p1, k1 tbl, p1, k1 tbl).

SQUARE BRACKETS

Some patterns have instructions given within square brackets. After the bracket it will tell you how many times to work that instruction in total. For example, [k3, p1 tbl] 3 times. This would be worked as k3, p1 tbl, k3, p1 tbl, k3, p1 tbl.

TECHNIQUES REFERENCE SOURCES

BOOKS

A good general knitting techniques book will be invaluable for helping you with some of the methods used in this book. We recommend **The Knitting Answer Book** by Margaret Radcliffe. ISBN 978-0715325759

ONLINE TUTORIALS

The internet is a great source of helpful tutorials and techniques videos. Here are some handy resources:

Knitting in the round is well-described in videos at KnittingHelp.com, which cover how to use double-pointed needles, two circular needles and the Magic Loop method **www.tinyurl.com/KnittingInTheRound**

The **long-tail cast-on method** shown on page 82 is shown in a video here: http://verypink.com/2010/03/13/video-long-tail-cast-on/

An **alternative long-tail cast-on** style is shown in a video at KnittingHelp.com: **www.tinyurl.com/CastOnMethods**

Kitchener stitch (grafting) (shown on page 81) is also covered in this article from Knitty.com: **www.tinyurl.com/KitchenerStitch**

CARE INSTRUCTIONS

Take care to follow the washing instructions on your ball band. Many sock yarns are machine washable at 40°C on a gentle cycle. Generally, hand-dyed yarns will keep their colours longer if they are hand-washed.

PATTERN QUERIES

If you think there may be an error with any of the pattern instructions, please email **coopknit@gmail.com**

KEEP IN TOUCH

My blog and online shop are at **www.coopknits.co.uk**

The Coop Knits group on Ravelry is friendly and funny. Please do join the group and share pictures of your Coop Knits projects. I love to see what you have been making. **www.ravelry.com/groups/coop-knits**

You can find me on Twitter and Instagram at **@CoopKnits** – don't forget to follow me, to keep up-to-date with new pattern releases.

How to...

AFTERTHOUGHT HEEL

This type of heel is used in the Orville sock pattern on page 22.

1. Return to the line of waste yarn that was knitted as part of the heel set-up instructions.

2. With RS facing, pick up the right leg of each stitch directly below the row of waste yarn. Use two DPNs, picking up half the total number of stitches on each needle.

3. Turn the sock and repeat Step 2, picking up the stitches on the other side of the waste yarn.

4. The stitches above and below the waste yarn are now spread across four DPNs. If using circular needles, pick up first side on needle tip, slide the stitches onto the cable, and pick up the second side on the needle tip.

5. Carefully remove the waste yarn, taking care that no stitches were missed from the picking up process.

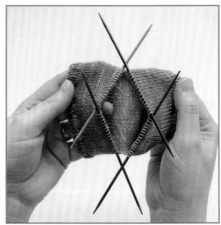

6. The live stitches are now spread across four DPNs and are ready to work.

KITCHENER STITCH (GRAFTING)

Every sock in this book uses Kitchener stitch to close the toe stitches. This tutorial shows you how, and gives tips on making the graft stitches neat and tidy.

1. Holding needles parallel to each other, thread a tapestry needle with the yarn tail. Insert the tapestry needle into the first stitch on the DPN closest to you **as if to purl** and pull it through, leaving the stitch **on** the needle.

2. Insert the needle into the first stitch on the DPN furthest from you **as if to knit** and pull it through, leaving the stitch **on** the needle.

3. Insert the needle into the first stitch on the DPN closest to you **as if to knit** and pull it through, slipping the stitch **off** the needle.

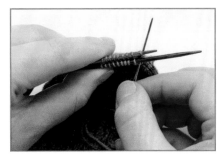

4. Insert the needle into the first stitch on the DPN closest to you **as if to purl** and pull it through, leaving the stitch **on** the needle.

5. Insert the needle into the first stitch on the DPN furthest from you **as if to purl** and pull it through, slipping the stitch **off** the needle.

6. Insert the needle into the first stitch on the DPN furthest from you **as if to knit** and pull it through, leaving the stitch **on** the needle.

FINISHING

Repeat steps 3-6 until all the live stitches have been grafted together.
The grafted stitches will be looser than the knitted stitches around them. Use the tapestry needle to neaten them: starting at the first stitch to be grafted, pull each stitch until it matches the knitted stitches on the toe. Take the yarn to the inside of the sock and weave in the end to finish.

LONG-TAIL CAST-ON

This cast-on method gives a firm but flexible edge that is perfect for socks.

1. Measure approximately 1m [1yd] of yarn, place the yarn over the needle with the ball at the rear and the tail of the yarn towards you. Use your forefinger to hold the yarn on the needle.

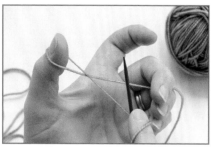

2. Using the tail end of the yarn, make a loop of yarn around your thumb as shown.

3. Put the needle tip into the loop.

4. Use your right hand to wrap the yarn from the ball side around the needle tip.

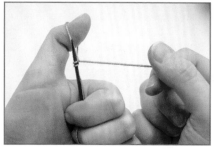

5. Use your thumb to lift the loop off the end of the needle, thus making the first (formed by holding the yarn over the needle) and second stitches.

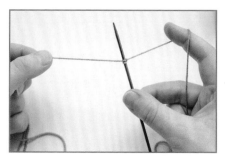

6. Gently tighten both ends of the yarn (tail and ball sides).

CONTINUE AS SET
Repeat steps 2 to 6 until you have cast on the desired number of stitches.

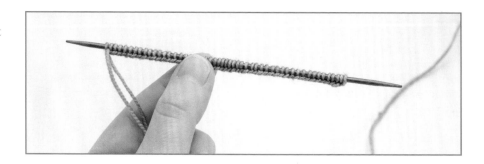

A good yarn

The yarns used for the socks in this book are all available to purchase online. Some are also available from good yarn shops. If you would like to substitute a different yarn for your socks, please do read the 'Choosing yarns' section on page 78, as well as checking your tension as you knit the first sock.

The list below shows where you can purchase the yarn I used for each sock design.

DAVE
Another Crafty Girl, Merino Sock
www.anothercraftygirl.com

EUGENE
Whimsy, Sokkusu O
www.whimzy.co.uk

PHYLLIS
Kettle Yarn Co, Twist
www.kettleyarnco.co.uk

ORVILLE
Lorna's Laces, Solemate
www.lornaslaces.net
Easyknits, Deeply Wicked
www.easyknits.co.uk

DECCA
John Arbon Textiles, Exmoor Sock Yarn
www.jarbon.com

DELBERT
Leading Men Fiber Arts, Spotlight
leadingmenfiberarts.bigcartel.com
Whimsy, Sokkkusu O
www.whimzy.co.uk

SIDNEY
Madelinetosh, Tosh Sock
www.madelinetosh.com

OTIS
The Knitting Goddess, Merino Nylon Sock Yarn
www.theknittinggoddess.co.uk

LAVERNE
The Knitting Goddess, Britsock Yarn
www.theknittinggoddess.co.uk

EULA
Blue Moon Fiber Arts, Socks That Rock Lightweight
www.bluemoonfiberarts.com

ERNESTINE
Babylonglegs, Flump Merino Sock
babylonglegs.bigcartel.com

WILBERT
Eden Cottage Yarns, Milburn 4ply
www.edencottageyarns.co.uk
Old Maiden Aunt, Superwash Merino
www.oldmaidenaunt.com

Abbreviations

1/1 LC	Slip next st to cable needle and place at front of work, k1, then k1 from cable needle
1/1 LKT	Slip next st to cable needle and place at front of work, k1, then k1tbl from cable needle
1/1 LPT	Slip next st to cable needle and place at front of work, p1, then k1tbl from cable needle
1/1 LT	Slip next st to cable needle and place at front of work, k1tbl, then k1tbl from cable needle
1/1 RC	Slip next st to cable needle and place at back of work, k1, then k1 from cable needle
1/1 RKT	Slip next st to cable needle and place at back of work, k1tbl, then k1 from cable needle
1/1 RPT	Slip next st to cable needle and place at back of work, k1tbl, then p1 from cable needle
1/1 RT	Slip next st to cable needle and place at back of work, k1tbl, then k1tbl from cable needle
1/1/1 LPT	Slip next 2 sts to cable needle and place at front of work, k1tbl, move last st from cable needle back on to left needle, p this st, k1tbl from cable needle
1/1/1 RPT	Slip next 2 sts to cable needle and place at back of work, k1tbl, move last st from cable needle back on to left needle, p this st, k1tbl from cable needle
2/1 LC	Slip next 2 sts to cable needle and place at front of work, k1, then k2 from cable needle
2/1 LPC	Slip next 2 sts to cable needle and place at front of work, p1, then k2 from cable needle
2/1 RC	Slip next st to cable needle and place at back of work, k2, then k1 from cable needle
2/1 RPC	Slip next st to cable needle and place at back of work, k2, then p1 from cable needle
2/1/2 LPC	Slip next 3 sts to cable needle and place at front of work, k2, move last st from cable needle back on to left needle, p this st, k2 from cable needle
2/1/2 RPC	Slip next 3 sts to cable needle and place at back of work, k2, move last st from cable needle back on to left needle, p this st, k2 from cable needle
2/2 LC	Slip next 2 sts to cable needle and place at front of work, k2, then k2 from cable needle
2/2 LKT	Slip next 2 sts to cable needle and place at front of work, k2, then k2tbl from cable needle
2/2 LPC	Slip next 2 sts to cable needle and place at front of work, p2, then k2 from cable needle
2/2 LPT	Slip next 2 sts to cable needle and place at front of work, p2, then k2tbl from cable needle
2/2 RC	Slip next 2 sts to cable needle and place at back of work, k2, then k2 from cable needle
2/2 RKT	Slip next 2 sts to cable needle and place at back of work, k2tbl, then k2 from cable needle

2/2 RPC	Slip next 2 sts to cable needle and place at back of work, k2, then p2 from cable needle
2/2 RPT	Slip next 2 sts to cable needle and place at back of work, k2tbl, then p2 from cable needle
3 st loop	Insert right needle into third st on left needle and draw this st over first 2 sts on left needle, and off the needle; k1, yo, k1.
CC	Contrast colour
cm	Centimetres
dec	Decreased
DPNs	Double-pointed needles
g	Grams
in	Inches
k	Knit
k2tog	Knit two stitches together as one stitch. 1 stitch decreased
m	Metres
m1 purlwise	Pick up the strand between stitches from front to back and purl through the back of this loop. 1 stitch increased
m1l	Pick up the strand between stitches from front to back and knit through the back of this loop. 1 stitch increased
m1r	Pick up the strand between stitches from back to front and knit this loop. 1 stitch increased
MC	Main colour
mm	Millimetres
p	Purl
p2tog	Purl two stitches together as one stitch. 1 stitch decreased
pm	Place marker
rep	Repeat
RS	Right side of work
sl	Slip the next stitch from left to right purlwise
slm	Slip marker
ssk	Slip 2 stitches individually as if to knit, then knit those 2 stitches together through the back loops. 1 stitch decreased
st st	Stocking stitch (US: Stockinette stitch) Knit every round, when working in the round
st(s)	Stitch(es)
tbl	Through the back loop
WS	Wrong side of work
wyib	With yarn in back
wyif	With yarn in front
yds	Yards
yo	Yarnover